PARTNERSHIP TAXATION
— a practical guide

STANTON MARCUS, FCA
and
CHRISTOPHER COX, BCL, MA(Oxon), Solicitor

Financial Techniques Limited
Woking Surrey

First Impression July 1976
Second Impression October 1977
Second Edition May 1979

ISBN 0 905583 01 1

Printed in England by
Signland Limited, Farnham, Surrey

CONTENTS

ABOUT THE AUTHORS

STANTON MARCUS heads the tax planning division of a City-based tax advisory company, and is widely recognised as an authority and leading communicator in this field. During 15 years in the City he has made a special study of tax saving strategies, especially for partnerships and has advised a wide range of business and professional organisations. He is Managing Editor of *Business Tax Quarterly*, a journal which provides positive action planning advice in the area of business tax.

CHRISTOPHER COX is a solicitor. He has specialised in tax consultancy and has extensive experience of advising partnerships. He also lectures on partnership tax matters and is a regular contributor to *Business Tax Quarterly.*

FOREWORD

If you are a typical partner in a typical firm there have probably been many occasions when you have said something like this: "I'm making much more money now than I was ten years ago but after paying tax I seem to have less than ever to spend."

The prime objective of this book is to give some help to remedy this depressing situation (exaggerated though it may be) by explaining to the non-expert reader some of the ways in which partnerships may be able to effect tax savings. Our other objective is to give useful practical guidance on the way in which partnership taxation works – not just to set out the rules in a dull and lifeless form, but to explain their effect on typical business situations.

Partnerships come in all shapes and sizes. The reader may be a member of a medium-sized firm of surveyors; or of a partnership owning a chain of shops; or a partner in an international firm of lawyers – the possibilities are limitless. We have tried to cater for all, but we suspect that the majority of our readers will be partners in professional firms. This explains why the many examples and case histories in the book are usually based on the circumstances of professional partnerships; non-professional readers should easily be able to translate the facts to apply to their own particular firms. We hope, by the way, that our professional readers will not feel hurt by the fact that in the book we use the word "business" to cover both professional and trading activities rather than the less descriptive term "practice"!

As you progress through the book, you will find that we have assumed that our readers have no previous knowledge of taxation, which is in our view just what authors of a readable practical guide should do. To those readers who are themselves experienced advisers on tax matters (we have in mind accountants and solicitors in particular) we express the hope that they will benefit from studying the subject with the particular practical slant which we have tried to give it. These experienced readers will recognise as they read the book that we have made no attempt to cover every aspect of the subject; to keep the book within reasonable limits we have been deliberately selective and we have chosen areas of major importance and where there are tax saving opportunities. We have assumed that our readers are more concerned with tax saving than with the many mathematical niceties of tax.

In short, we have attempted in this book to dissolve some of the mystique surrounding the subject of partnership taxation. We hope we have been reasonably successful.

Stanton Marcus

Hillgate House
Old Bailey
London EC4

May 1979

A NOTE TO THE TECHNICAL READER

To enable readers and their advisers to investigate particular partnership taxation problems in greater depth, the text of this book is supplemented by a Technical Supplement.

To avoid the distraction of conventional footnotes, the Technical Supplement is set out at the end of the book just before the index. This supplement incorporates statutory and case references and the reader is recommended to consult it whenever he has a particular technical interest in the contents of the chapter.

The law is stated as at 1 May 1979.

On 3 April 1979 the Chancellor of the Exchequer gave us a "holding" budget. He announced certain increases in the personal allowances for income tax but said that otherwise the tax rates for 1979/80 would be the same as for 1978/79. There will however be a full budget after the general election and it is likely that the rates of income tax for 1979/80 will be changed then. Therefore when we show how partners' tax bills are worked out in Chapter 10 we take 1978/79 as our specimen year.

CHAPTER ONE

PARTNERSHIP TAXATION – AN INTRODUCTORY SKETCH

This book about partnership taxation is designed to be easily used at a practical level. The first thing to be done therefore is to show in simple outline form what the structure of partnership tax looks like in practice. Let us start by considering the straightforward situation of a small firm of architects; the two partners, Stan and Ollie, take one-half of the profits each. We will assume that the firm prepares its business accounts each year up to 30 June and that the profit shown by the accounts for the year ending 30 June 1977 is £40,000.

Before developing our examination of these facts, two points need to be made to reassure the reader. Firstly, the straightforward situation of a two-man partnership, rather than something more complicated, has been deliberately adopted in the interests of simplicity of explanation. The principles that are about to be discussed will apply to your own firm even though it has many more partners and a more complex structure than the firm of Stan & Ollie. Or, for that matter, even if it has the simpler structure of a one-man business. (This applies generally to the examples and illustrations throughout this book). Similarly, the figures used in this illustration (and in the others in this book) are hypothetical; the principles discussed apply, in general, regardless of the range in which your own firm's profit falls.

The second point of reassurance for the reader is that this opening illustration is designed principally to set the scene for detailed discussion in later chapters of this book. Readers should not therefore allow themselves to become concerned or puzzled about any detailed aspects of the brief explanations given in the first part of this chapter. Full explanations will be given subsequently.

There are several stages in calculating the tax payable by the firm of Stan & Ollie from its business accounts for the year ending 30 June 1977. They can be summarised as follows:-

Stage 1	Profit shown by business accounts for year ending 30 June 1977	£40,000
Stage 2	Profit adopted for tax purposes for year ending 30 June 1977	£34,000
Stage 3	Income tax payable for the year ending 5 April 1979 on £34,000	£12,629.50

This simple outline has shown that the business accounts for the year ending 30 June 1977 have undergone two changes for tax purposes: stage 2 above indicates that the profit shown by the accounts is adjusted to a different figure before it becomes suitable for taxation; and stage 3 shows that the year ending 30 June 1977 is, somewhat mysteriously, converted to the year ending 5 April 1979. These two important changes are fully discussed in subsequent chapters of this book; the structure is broadly as follows:

> The way in which the profit shown by the accounts amounting to £40,000 is converted to a taxable figure of £34,000 is explained in chapters 2 and 3 (with subsidiary explanation of certain special aspects in some later chapters).
>
> The way in which the year ending 30 June 1977 is converted to the year ending 5 April 1979 and the vital practical consequences of this change are explained in chapter 4.
>
> Chapter 10 explains how the firm's income tax liability

of £12,629.50 is calculated from the figure of £34,000.

The remaining chapters cover a number of special aspects of taxation of interest to partnerships.

Although the purpose of this opening chapter has been principally to provide a simple illustrative background for the detailed discussion that follows in the rest of the book, there are two questions that can usefully be dealt with now. Readers will have seen that the amount of tax payable on the £40,000 profit made in the year ending 30 June 1977 is £12,629.50. How does this profit figure tie in with the "drawings" extracted by the individual partners from the firm? And who has the responsibility of paying the tax to the Inland Revenue?

Partners' Drawings

In a typical partnership, each of the individual partners will draw a fixed sum regularly from the firm, usually referred to as "drawings". For example, consider Stan in the Stan & Ollie partnership: perhaps he draws £750 per month. His drawings will amount to £9,000 in the year ending 30 June 1977. At the end of the year when his partnership profit share is calculated, the £9,000 will be deducted in calculating the amount due to him; any further sum then paid to him is also classified as drawings. Many partners are confused over tax and drawings, so here is a brief explanation.

There is no tax on drawings as such. Stan does not pay any tax on his regular £750 per month or on any other drawings. But when, at the end of the year, the firm's profit is calculated, no deduction from profit is allowed by the Inland Revenue for partners' drawings. One way of looking at this is to say that income tax on drawings is effectively included in the firm's income tax paid on its profits.

In a nutshell, the amount of the partners' drawings has no effect on the calculation of the firm's income tax. A prosperous 12-man partnership may make a profit of, say, £500,000 but, because money has to be ploughed back into the firm to finance expansion and inflationary increases, the twelve partners may be able to draw only

£80,000 between them. Income tax on the firm will be calculated on the £500,000; the fact that the amount available for drawings is much lower is totally ignored. This is a major feature of the system of taxing partnerships. It is worth pointing out briefly at this stage that *companies* are dealt with rather differently — this will be fully developed in chapter 11.

Who is Liable for Partnership Tax?

Tax law lays down that the income tax assessment on the partnership business profits shall be made jointly in the name of the partnership. The general rules of partnership law provide that every partner in a firm is liable jointly with the other partners for all debts and obligations of the firm incurred while he is a partner. The practical result is that the Inland Revenue will claim the tax of £12,629.50 from the firm of Stan & Ollie and, if the firm does not pay the tax, the Inland Revenue can proceed for the whole of the tax against any one of the individual partners. They could, for example, demand the whole of the £12,629.50 from Ollie in the event that Stan was unable or unwilling to pay his share.

The consequences are even more extreme in a larger firm. Going back to the 12-man partnership, the Inland Revenue are entitled to proceed for the whole of the tax against any one or more of the partners. In theory (but, of course, it would rarely occur in practice), the Inland Revenue could proceed for the whole of the tax against, say, two junior partners each of whom had only a 2½% share!

The 12-man partnership example is probably fanciful but there is an important practical lesson in all this. Some firms are in the happy position of sitting on a mountain of surplus cash. One often finds that partnerships in this enviable situation prepare their annual business accounts, calculate the share of profit to which each partner is entitled and then pay each partner his appropriate share after deducting drawings already made by the partner during the year. Any firms that do this or something like this should realise that they are in peril of one partner not being able to pay his share of the partnership income tax. Before paying away profit-shares to partners it obviusly makes good sense to hold something back to meet income tax. With income tax rates on professional and trade profits reaching a maximum at the present time of as much as 83% (more about this in chapter 10), it is foolhardy not to make retentions from partners' profit-shares to meet income tax. Especially where there is likely to be a delay in agreeing the tax bill with the Inland Revenue.

And Now a Different Tax

The discussion so far in this chapter has related to income tax. It is well known that apart from tax being payable on business profits (income tax) there is a further tax on profits made on the disposal of capital assets (capital gains tax). What is not always realised is that capital gains tax is a largely self-contained system of taxation which is totally distinct from income tax; the two taxes are not two branches of one form of tax. The practical importance of this remark is that, by and large, income tax rules have no bearing on capital gains tax.

A discussion of the wide-ranging and complex system of capital gains tax is outside the scope of a publication of this size and nature, but in the context of this chapter it is worth pointing out that capital gains tax on any capital profit made by a partnership is not assessed jointly in the name of the firm. Each individual partner will personally be charged tax by the Inland Revenue on his proportionate share of the partnership's capital profit.

Chapter 1 – The Warning Repeated

Income tax on business profits is a joint liability of the partnership. Do not allow the partners in your firm to draw out their shares of profit without leaving money in the partnership to pay for the tax. Remember that for high-earning partners the overall tax rate may be considerable.

CHAPTER TWO
HOW PARTNERSHIP PROFITS ARE CALCULATED FOR TAX
PART 1 – IS ALL MONEY RECEIVED LIABLE TO TAX?

Introduction

In chapter 1, we saw that the amount of profit shown by the accounts of the Stan & Ollie partnership was adjusted before it became an acceptable figure for tax purposes. The profit of £40,000 became £34,000 for tax purposes, although the adjustment could equally have gone the other way producing a profit for tax of, say, £43,000. There are a very large number of rules which set out the adjustments to be made for tax and in this chapter we begin our consideration of these rules.

The subject of computing profits for tax purposes is a very large one and this practical guide can do no more than discuss general approaches to the problem; the authors do not pretend that they cover everything. In this chapter we shall consider the income side of the partnership profit and loss account and in the next chapter the expenditure side.

A number of special aspects which have a bearing on the calculation of profits for tax are dealt with in subsequent chapters in this book; notably, chapters 6 and 7 deal with the tax allowances for depreciation and chapter 8 explains the special tax reliefs attaching to professional work-in-progress and trade stock. It is important to emphasise that in the various chapters of this book dealing with the calculation of profits, the discussion is directed solely towards what might be termed partnership business profits; the discussion has no application to the calculation of partnership capital gains, in regard to which special rules exist which are outside the scope of this particular book.

Partnership Income

In practice, relatively few difficult problems arise on the question of whether an amount of money received by a partnership is taxable as income or not. A professional partnership will receive fees from its clients and a trading or manufacturing partnership will receive money in respect of its sales to its customers and it is rare for these items to be the subject of disagreement with the Inland Revenue.

Where difficulty does sometimes arise is on those occasions when a partnership receives a gratuitous sum from one of its clients or customers. We shall shortly examine a practical case history involving a firm of chartered accountants who received an unsolicited sum of money from one of their clients. Before this is done, it is useful to postulate a rule which can be regarded as fundamental in calculating profits for tax purposes.

The Fundamental Rule

The tax statutes direct that income tax is to be charged on "the full amount of the profits or gains" of the partnership business. Because the word "profits" is to be given its natural meaning, the figure of profit to be adopted for tax purposes is in the first instance to be calculated on ordinary commercial principles of accountancy.

The fundamental rule may therefore be expressed as follows: for income tax purposes, profits are initially to be calculated on ordinary commercial principles of accountancy. But after they have been calculated in this way they are to be adjusted according to the special tax rules (some of which are described in subsequent chapters of this book). The fundamental rule is very often of considerable use in solving problems relating to the calculation of partnership profits as will be shown by the practical case history that follows.

Case History 2.1

This is a simplified version of events that actually occurred to a firm of chartered accountants, Carnaby Harrower, Barham & Pykett. The case concerns an amount of £2,567 which they received from one of their clients in special circumstances. The facts in this case history have been condensed from the report of the Court case between Carnaby and the Inspector of Taxes in 1969.

Carnaby had acted as auditors to the Motor Union Insurance Co Ltd and five of its associated companies until the year 1963. In 1963, Carnaby were asked by Motor Union not to seek re-appointment and they agreed to this. This step was explained to the Motor Union shareholders in the directors' report issued with the 1962 accounts as follows:

> Messrs Carnaby Harrower, Barham & Pykett, Chartered Accountants, do not offer themselves for re-election as auditors of the company. With the integration of the head office departments on a group basis it has become increasingly difficult for many aspects of the audit to be conducted on a company basis. Messrs Price Waterhouse & Co, Chartered Accountants, who are the auditors of the parent company, have therefore been invited to assume the duties of auditors of the company and have expressed their willingness to serve in that capacity.
>
> The directors desire to pay a warm tribute to the retiring auditors for their valued services to the company over a period of twenty-seven years.

In May 1963, Carnaby submitted invoices for their charges amounting to £2,567 in connection with the 1962 audit and these invoices were duly paid. In August 1963, Carnaby received from Motor Union a second cheque for £2,567 together with the following letter:

> Dear Sirs, At the annual general meeting of the company held on 23 May 1963, at which date you vacated the office of auditors, a warm tribute was paid to your firm for your valued services to our group of companies over such a long period of years and I have now been instructed by the directors to forward to you a cheque from the companies mentioned below for the sum of £2,567 as solatium for

the loss of the office of auditors. In enclosing this cheque I would like to take the opportunity of adding my personal thanks for your help and advice over the past few years.

Company	Amount of Solatium
The Motor Union Insurance Co Ltd	£1,239
Car & General Insurance Corp Ltd	1,176
Car Services Ltd	52
The C & G Group Pension Fund	52
Car Corp of Gt Britain Ltd	16
Royex Investment Co Ltd	32

The Court was asked to decide whether the second cheque received by Carnaby in August 1963 was taxable as part of the income of their business. It will be noticed that the second cheque was entirely unsolicited by Carnaby but that it was made payable to the firm and not to any one or more partners personally. The Court applied the fundamental rule explained earlier in this chapter and decided that the amount was not taxable. The Court said that because the second cheque was voluntary and was not paid as consideration for past services, it was not part of the business profits calculated on ordinary commercial principles of accountancy. It was therefore not liable to tax.

Gratuitous Receipts

Now you may have difficulty in accepting the principle of the Court's reasoning in the Carnaby Harrower case and you may think that it conflicts with business commonsense but, as will appear at other points in this book, commonsense has little or no application in solving tax problems! In any event, who is going to carp at a decision that demonstrates that some partnership receipts may be tax-free? In the authors' experience, it is not uncommon to find a partnership receiving a voluntary payment from a client or customer and few partnerships realise that it can often be argued that these amounts are not part of the business profits of the firm and are not liable to tax.

CHAPTER TWO

TAX MITIGATION CHECK-LIST

Has your firm received some gratuitous amount from a client or customer, over and above the normal fee or charge, by way of consolation on the termination of a contract or by way of recognition of (rather than reward for) past services? If so, put forward the argument that, on ordinary commercial principles of accountancy, the gratuitous receipt is not part of business taxable profits.

CHAPTER THREE
HOW PARTNERSHIP PROFITS ARE CALCULATED FOR TAX
PART II – WHAT EXPENSES ARE ALLOWED FOR TAX?

What This Chapter Will Tell You

When a partner is faced with a partnership expense, he will normally decide whether it is allowable for tax by turning his mind to whether the expenditure could in fairness be described as a legitimate business expense, or whether he could prove that the firm's business has obtained some benefit from the expenditure. But when he consults his tax advisers he will be told, often to his surprise, that nowhere in tax legislation is there a reference to "legitimate business expenditure" or to the benefit produced by business expenses.

In the first part of this chapter, the *general* rules for tax allowability of expenditure are described so that the partner can have some idea of the reasons for replies given by his tax adviser to questions regarding allowable expenses.

After the description of the general rules, there follows a review of the tax legislation relating to some *specific* items of expenditure. To help the reader make his own tentative decision on the allowability of any items of expenditure, the chapter ends with a summary in the form of a simplified decision chart. The chart is intended to be used as no more than a general guide. Difficult borderline questions will require expert advice.

The authors repeat the important comments made in the introduction to chapter 2: no attempt has been made to cover every aspect of this far-reaching subject; and the discussion relates to expenses allowable against business profits and not to capital gains, where special rules apply.

Ground Rules for Partnership Expenses

In determining whether or not an item of expenditure is allowable for tax there are a number of separate hurdles to be overcome. Broadly, these can be stated in the form of three general questions. The answers to all three questions must be 'yes' before the expenditure can be deducted for tax purposes. The questions will form the basis of the detailed discussion in this chapter and they are incorporated in the decision chart at the end of this chapter. Some readers may find that it assists them if they make occasional reference to the decision chart while studying the detailed discussion that follows. Briefly, the three questions are:

1. On ordinary accounting principles is it a proper business expense? (This is another application of the fundamental rule explained in the previous chapter.)

2. Is the amount expended wholly and exclusively for the purpose of the partnership's business?

3. Is the expense of a revenue nature and not capital expenditure?

This third question often causes confusion in the mind of the business partner. His reasoning runs rather like this: if expenditure is of a revenue nature (for example, rent, salaries and other day-to-day running expenses) it will be allowed in full as a deduction this year. And if it is capital (for example, office equipment and business cars) it will be allowed in full by way of tax depreciation allowances, spread possibly over this year and future years. Why then, he asks himself, should it matter whether for tax purposes expenditure is classified as revenue or capital apart from the obvious effect on the timing of tax allowances?

But in many instances, it does matter. Later in this chapter and again in chapter 6, it will be explained that many items of capital expenditure do not in fact qualify for any tax depreciation allowances. The distinction between revenue and capital expenditure is a very important one for this reason. It is, of course, important also for the effect on cash flow resulting from the timing of some of the depreciation allowances.

As a final check on the allowability of expenditure, a fourth specific question must be asked:

4. Is it specifically disallowed by tax legislation?

If the answer to this question is 'yes' then of course the expenditure must be disallowed even though it passes the first three general tests.

Each of these four questions is now considered in detail.

Ordinary Accounting Principles

If the expenditure is deductible according to the ordinary principles of commercial accountancy then, provided it meets the other general tests for allowable expenditure and is not specifically disallowed by tax legislation, it must be allowed for tax purposes. This rule tends to overlap the question posed at 3 above (that is, is it revenue or capital?) and that aspect will be examined later in this chapter. Apart from this a simple example of the application of ordinary accounting principles to tax can be seen in the allowance of expenses that have "accrued" during the year but fall due for payment after the end of the year. End-of-year bonuses paid to staff under a profit-sharing scheme are an excellent illustration of this: if they "accrue" in year 1 and are paid in year 2 they are allowed in year 1. Ordinary accounting prnciples dictate that the bonuses are a proper expense in year 1. An expense does not fall at the first of the three hurdles listed above simply because it has accrued rather than been paid.

The importance of accounting principles was emphasised forcefully by Lord Clyde in the case of Lothian Chemical Co Ltd v. Rogers which was heard as long ago as 1926. Lord Clyde said:

"It has been said times without number ... you deal in the

> main with ordinary principles of commercial accounting. They (the tax statutes) do expressly exclude a number of deductions and allowances, some of which according to the principles of commercial accounting might be allowable. But where the ordinary principles are not invaded by statute they must be allowed to prevail."

A problem is, of course, *who* decides whether the expenditure is deductible according to the normal principles of commercial accounting? The short answer is that it is the Courts who decide with the aid of evidence from accountants. Accountants are not the complete masters; their evidence is in no way conclusive. In the 1972 case of Heather v P.E. Consulting Group Ltd, Lord Denning M.R. referring to the status of accountancy evidence said:

> "The Courts have always been assisted greatly by the evidence of accountants. Their practice should be given due weight; but the Courts have never regarded themselves as being bound by it. It would be wrong to do so."

Therefore, whilst accountancy evidence is an important aid to the Courts, the Courts reserve their right to either accept or reject that evidence.

The "Wholly and Exclusively" test

The phrase "wholly and exclusively" used in the second of the four questions is familiar to all who are connected with business taxation. There has been a rule for over 130 years preventing the deduction of expenses from business income unless the expenditure is wholly and exclusively for business purposes.

The phrase "wholly and exclusively for business purposes" is attractively simple but the simplicity is deceptive. Over the last century the Courts have had to consider many borderline cases in order to decide whether they fell within the "wholly and exclusively" test. The practical case history that follows is a good illustration of the application of the "wholly and exclusively" test. The particular facts of the case are also of special interest in the field of partnership taxation.

Case History 3.1

This case raises the question of the allowability for tax of the cost of attending professional conferences abroad. The costs consisted of hotel and travelling expenses. The case is a simplified version of an actual Court hearing in 1965.

Russell & Russell, a firm of solicitors in Bolton, had a sole principal at the time with which we are here concerned (1960), a Mr Taylor. Mr Taylor visited the United States and Canada for about four weeks in August and September of 1960 in order to attend the annual meeting of the American Bar Association and the Ottawa Law Conference.

His journey was arranged by the Law Society in London and the total cost was £573. About one half of this total was travelling expenses and the other half hotels and meals.

Although he was accompanied by his wife he was careful to charge in the accounts of his practice only his own expenditure. The amount of £573 included nothing in respect of Mrs Taylor.

The claim for a deduction from the profits of Russell & Russell was rejected by the Inspector of Taxes and the case came before the Appeal Commissioners, that is, the independent tribunal whose task it is to hear tax disputes. At the hearing, Mr Taylor was asked what he did in the United States and Canada and he replied that he attended five conference sessions on legal subjects and he visited local lawyers and examined their methods. He also added (although this was fairly obvious) that he went sightseeing with his wife.

Now although it is useful to know what Mr Taylor did while he was in the United States and Canada it is of much greater importance in deciding whether the expenditure is allowable to consider his precise motive in making the visits. This is because of the form of words used in the "wholly and exclusively" test. The word "purposes" in the test indicates that the dominant feature to be taken into account in deciding whether the "wholly and exclusively" test is complied with is the motive or object in the mind of the taxpayer when the expenditure is incurred.

Before the Appeal Commissioners Mr Taylor was therefore questioned as to his motive in making the visits. The main part of his answer to this question was to point out that there were three reasons for his attending the conferences. They were, he said, to maintain his status as a solicitor, to improve his reputation in the United Kingdom and to increase his clientele. So far, so good.

But he then gave the Appeal Commissioners a further piece of information which, for reasons that will soon be clear, had a great bearing on the result of the case. He said that it was also his intention to have a holiday with his wife at the same time.

The Appeal Commissioners allowed the claim for the hotel and travelling expenses except for a round sum of £125 in respect of the expenditure on meals. The Inland Revenue appealed to the High Court. There they put forward two alternative bases on which to reject the claim. The first of these was that the nature of the conferences was too remote from the practice of Russell & Russell. The firm was not an international one but conducted a general legal practice in Lancashire and it was suggested that the conference expenses therefore had only a remote connection with the practice and could not be allowed. The Court, as we shall see, expressed no point of view on this argument.

The second and alternative argument by the Inland Revenue was that the expenditure had a dual motive. The purpose of the expenditure (and this, it will be recalled, is the true test) was not only to attend the conferences but also to have a holiday. It is worth noticing at this point that the word used by Mr Taylor when he said that it was also his "intention" to have a holiday is very close to the word "purposes" used in the test.

Clearly then, on his own admission, Mr Taylor had not fallen entirely within the "wholly and exclusively" test. On any commonsense or equitable approach therefore one would assume that the expenses of £573 would be apportioned between deductible professional expenses and non-deductible personal expenses. But this was not the result of the case.

Because Mr Taylor had admitted that there was some non-professional motive in the expenditure it was impossible to say that the expense was "wholly and *exclusively*" incurred for the purposes of his profession. The *whole* of it therefore fell outside the test and no part could be allowed.

The rule is summed up in one sentence in the judgement

of the High Court: "But once it is found that the person has a distinct purpose other than that of enabling him to carry on and earn profits in his trade or profession ...... (the wholly and exclusively test) prohibits deduction of the expense."

The Court quashed the claim completely on the grounds of duality of motive and it was therefore unnecessary for the Court to consider the alternative Inland Revenue argument that the expenditure was too remote.

Duality of Motive

The important practical effect of the Russell & Russell case is that it demonstrates that where a partnership has incurred expenditure with a dual motive (that is, partly a business motive and partly a non-business motive), then, unless the expenditure is clearly divisible by its very nature (more about this a little later), there can be no apportionment and the whole amount will be disallowed against profits, however illogical the results of doing that may be.

But all is not gloom! If it can be truthfully be said that the *sole* objective for a particular item of expenditure (overseas travel is a good example) is the promotion of the business then the expenditure is not to be disallowed for tax simply because its nature necessarily involves some personal enjoyment or satisfaction by the partner undertaking the expenditure. It is wrong to think that anything that is enjoyable cannot also be allowable! On the other hand, if the expenditure is undertaken partly with the object of providing personal enjoyment then no part of it is allowable for tax purposes. The line between these two concepts is, admittedly, finely drawn and in practice therefore the method of presentation of the argument is of paramount importance.

Divisible Expenditure

In the discussion above of the Russell & Russell case, reference was made to the fact that the no-apportionment rule would not apply where the expenditure was by its very nature divisible between business purposes and non-business purposes. For example, in the 1941 case of Copeman v. William Flood & Sons Ltd, two young directors of the particular company (aged 17 and 23 years) had minor duties

It is wrong to think that anything that is enjoyable cannot also be allowable

as a telephonist and a buyer respectively. Each received £2,600 as director's fees in the accounts for the year ended 30 April 1938. These amounts are substantial by today's standards let alone those of 1938 and readers will not be surprised to learn that the two young directors were the children of the controlling shareholder! In view of the ages and duties of the two directors the Court held that the fees paid were excessive. Accordingly, the total fees were divided and only that part which was genuinely expended "wholly and exclusively" for the purposes of the company's trade was allowed.

Although the William Flood & Sons decision related to a limited company, the same principle will apply to partnerships. If the Inland Revenue can demonstrate that salaries paid by the firm to, for example, wives and children of the partners are excessive by reference to a comparison with salaries paid to outsiders then the partnership must expect to have a deduction for the salaries challenged. Only a reasonable market salary will be allowed.

Reference to divisible expenditure was also made in the 1975 case of Caillebotte v. Quinn. In that case, Mr Justice Templeman referred to the situation where a partner or a sole trader or practitioner used a room in his home partly as a business study and partly for leisure. In his judgment he made the useful comment:

"But it is possible to apportion the use and cost of the room on a time basis, and to allow the expense of the room during the hours in which it is used exclusively for business purposes, in the same way as it is possible to calculate the business expenses of a car which is sometimes used for business purposes exclusively and sometimes used for pleasure."

Pre-business and Post-business Expenses

When the "wholly and exclusively" test talks of business purposes it means, broadly speaking, a business that is currently functioning at the time the expenditure is incurred. Where a partnership incurs expenditure before its business commences (for example, a newly formed partnership that pays rent for an office some weeks before it actually begins to operate) the expenditure, in strict law, cannot be said to be for the purposes of its business. Similarly, if expenditure is incurred after a partnership business has ceased (perhaps "golden handshakes" to staff members after a firm has completely closed its business) it is not wholly and exclusively for the purposes of the business. Hence in both these cases the expenditure will be disallowed – examples of how tax law is forever splitting hairs! (But see the paragraph "Redundancy payments" towards the end of this chapter.)

Is it Revenue and Not Capital?

Proceeding with our discussion of the four questions listed at the beginning of this chapter and incorporated in the decision chart, question 3 must be asked because of the long established rule of tax law that if expenditure is to be allowed it must be revenue and not capital. Before we launch off on our detailed examination of this particular question, it may help those readers who are totally unfamiliar with the subject if a brief word or two is provided about the terminology being used. In preparing business accounts, accountants divide expenditure very broadly into two categories: first, expenses of the day-to-day running of the business; and, second, expenses which increase the assets of the business. The terminology used for these two categories (which is adopted also in discussion of the income tax aspects of the problem) needs to be understood before we proceed. The first category of expenditure is usually referred to as revenue expenditure or, sometimes, as expenditure of an income nature (this is a particularly baffling phrase for the uninitiated!). The second category is called capital expenditure.

Now although income tax uses the same terminology as accountants in classifying expenditure, it sometimes adopts different tests from those used by accountants in deciding on which side of the line expenditure falls. And this is where the trouble begins. It might be thought that provided the expense item is a proper expense for accountancy purposes, in accordance with question 1 in the list at the beginning of this chapter, then it is automatically revenue and not capital. This is not so. Although its accountancy treatment will in many cases be an important factor in deciding whether an item of expenditure is capital or revenue the final result is a question of law to be decided by the Courts.

What is Capital Expenditure? – An Old Established Income Tax Test

The tax legislation does not define capital expenditure but the test often applied for income tax is that given by Lord Cave in 1926 in Atherton v. British Insulated and Helsby Cables Ltd:

> "When an expenditure is made, not only once and for all, but with a view to bringing into existence an asset or an advantage for the enduring benefit of a trade ... there is very good reason (in the absence of special circumstances leading to an opposite conclusion) for treating such an expenditure as properly attributable not to revenue but to capital."

In general, therefore, expenditure incurred "with a view to bringing into existence an asset or an advantage for the enduring benefit of a trade" is capital expenditure. This obviously includes expenditure on the acquisition of equipment, plant, office machinery and buildings, and for many of these items tax depreciation allowances are given (as will be explained in chapters 6 and 7) but the borderline between capital and revenue expenditure is often difficult to ascertain.

An interesting practical example of a borderline case where the British Insulated principle was applied is the 1946 case of

Associated Portland Cement Manufacturers Ltd v. Kerr. Two directors of the company retired and signed agreements not to compete with the company after their retirement. The company paid them £30,000 as consideration for the agreements. The Courts decided that the payment brought into existence an advantage for the enduring benefit of the company's trade. The payment was therefore capital and was not allowable. This application of the British Insulated principle highlights its practical importance and is rather startling in its inequity since the £30,000 did not, of course, qualify for tax depreciation allowances so that no tax relief at all was obtained for this expense. This decision would apply equally if the payments were made by a partnership instead of a limited company.

The Associated Portland Cement case amply illustrates two points made earlier in this and the previous chapter. First, that there are items of expenditure which are treated as capital for income tax and therefore not allowable, but which do not qualify for tax depreciation allowances – they fall between two stools and provide no tax relief at all to the payer. Second, that business commonsense has no application to tax problems!

What is Capital Expenditure? – A Modern Income Tax View

Tax law does not stand still and in the fifty years or so since Lord Cave stated the test for capital expenditure referred to earlier, the Courts have been called upon time and time again to consider the distinction between capital and revenue in the light of particular circumstances. This has sometimes resulted in judges making statements which add a gloss to Lord Cave's test. And in some instances the Courts have put forward new tests of general application.

Some very useful remarks were made relatively recently by Mr Justice Megarry in the case of Pitt v. Castle Mill Warehousing Co Ltd. This case was heard in 1974 and concerned a company which had incurred expenditure in replacing an access road to one of its warehouses, in rather special circumstances. The company and the Inland Revenue disagreed over whether, for tax purposes, the expenditure was capital or revenue. The company lost as the Court decided that the expenditure was capital. The precise facts of the case are relatively unimportant for the purposes of the present discussion; what does matter is that Mr Justice Megarry put forward a useful three-part approach to the problem. He referred in his judgement to some previous cases heard by the Courts on the subject in recent years and he said that these cases established that in determining whether a payment is revenue or capital for income tax one must consider at least three elements:

> "First, what is the nature of the payment? Is there a single non-recurrent lump sum, paid once-for-all, on the one hand, or are there to be current payments, made, for example, for periods commensurate with those payments?
>
> "Second, what is to be obtained by the payment? Is it some asset with lasting or enduring qualities, or is it merely ephemeral, or, indeed, something which cannot be described as an asset, whether tangible or intangible?
>
> "Third, in what manner is what is obtained to be used, relied on or enjoyed? Will it have a quality of recurrence which will point to an income nature, as by providing the flow of orders for goods, or will it bear a static aspect which points to a capital nature?
>
> "In considering all these elements, and in looking at the case as a whole, it is the practical and business point of view that counts for more than the juristic classification of the legal rights employed or exhausted in the process."

The distinction between revenue expenditure and capital expenditure has a far-reaching effect on the calculation of partnership profits. The three-part test referred to in the above judgement will often be of great help in solving practical problems.

The tax cases and principles described so far illustrate the considerable problems confronting professional tax advisers in distinguishing between capital and revenue expenditure. It has already been mentioned that although expenditure which is branded as capital will be disallowed in calculating taxable profits a tax depreciation allowance may sometimes be available. Tax depreciation allowances are discussed in chapters 6 and 7 and it will be noted from chapter 6 that *some* capital expenditure is eligible for a 100% allowance in the year in which the expenditure is incurred. In these cases, where the expenditure qualifies for a 100% write-off, the argument between what is capital and what is revenue becomes largely academic.

Are Repairs Ever Capital?

A problem that has been around for some time and which is often met in partnership businesses is the question of what is often known as "initial repairs". Suppose that a partnership takes new premises in March 1979 and, before the partnership commences to use the premises for business purposes or, perhaps, shortly afterwards it spends £2,000 on redecorations and repairs. Are these "initial repairs" capital expenditure and therefore not allowable?

For very many years past the Inland Revenue have taken the view that initial repairs are capital expenditure following a decision in 1923 called Inland Revenue v. Law Shipping Co Ltd. But more recently the position has altered as a result of the 1971 case of Odeon Associated Theatres Ltd v. Jones. It is useful to make a comparison between these two important cases both for the purpose of deciding what is the present legal position with regard to initial repairs and because they throw some more light on the old problem of "capital v. revenue".

Briefly, the details of these two cases are as follows:

1. Inland Revenue v Law Shipping Co Ltd (1923)
   This case related to a ship which had been sent on a voyage when repairs certified as due on a Lloyds Survey had not been carried out. The vessel came into new ownership just before this voyage and the new owners carried out the overdue repairs immediately the voyage was over. The Inspector of Taxes refused a deduction for these repairs, claiming that they were capital expenditure mainly because the ship would have cost more if it had been put into a proper state of repair before it changed hands. The Inspector's view was upheld in the Courts. The repairs were not an allowable

expense. (But, fortunately for the company, tax depreciation allowances would have been claimable on the repair expenditure.)

2. Odeon Associated Theatres Ltd v. Jones (1971)
   In this case, the company was the owner of a number of cinemas, and during and shortly after the last war it purchased additional cinemas on which maintenance and repairs had been neglected by reason of the war. The company had to function with its existing and newly-acquired properties in a somewhat run-down condition.

   The Regal Cinema, Marble Arch, was referred to as a typical case. It was bought by the company in 1945 for £240,000 and the subsequent cost of carrying out the repairs considered to be due at the date of acquisition was nearly £8,000. (This would have been allowed without question if the ownership had not changed.)

   A start on carrying out the deferred repairs was made in 1947 and the last of these repairs was completed only in 1954. The Inspector of Taxes rejected the company's claim that the cost of the repairs was allowable as a revenue expense because of the decision in the Law Shipping case. He contended that as the repairs related to the previous ownership of the cinema the expenditure was capital and not revenue. This was of great practical importance to Odeon because much of the expenditure on deferred repairs would not qualify for tax depreciation allowances if it were to be classified as capital. (As will be seen in chapter 7, capital expenditure on cinema buildings does not qualify.) The Courts, however, found in favour of the company and allowed the repairs as a revenue expense.

Law Shipping and Odeon Contrasted
From a detailed study of the judgments in the above two cases, three important differences emerge. They are:

1. In the Odeon Theatres case, evidence was given and

accepted that in accordance with the ordinary principles of accounting all repairs, including deferred repairs, should properly be charged as revenue expenditure. No such evidence was given in the Law Shipping case.

2. In the Law Shipping case, the purchase price for the ship was substantially less than it would have been if the repairs had been completed by the vendor. In the Odeon Theatres case, the purchase price was in no way affected by the state of poor repair of the cinema at the date of purchase.

3. The ship in the Law Shipping case was virtually unseaworthy at the date of purchase. Expenditure on repairs *had* to be carried out before the ship became a profit-earning asset. This was not so in the Odeon Theatres case where the cinema acquired was profit-earning at the date of purchase in spite of its state of disrepair. This difference was emphasised in the timing of the repairs. The ship in the Law Shipping case had to be repaired almost immediately after acquisition. By comparison the repairs in the Odeon Theatres case were carried out over a period after the date of purchase.

Repairs – The Lessons Summarised

In the light of the Odeon decision, the tax climate for initial repairs is now completely different from what it was about seven years ago. The very long established Inland Revenue practice of disallowing all initial repairs to premises should now be strongly resisted.

It seems probable that the Inland Revenue could only successfully argue that initial repairs are capital in one of three situations. First, where the premises or other asset was not in working order (to use simple language) at the time it changed hands and where the new owner or occupier has to put it into working order before being able to use it in his business. This was the case with Law Shipping Co Ltd but not so with Odeon Associated Theatres.

Second, where a capital sum has been paid for the premises (or would normally have been paid) and this has been reduced to take account of the poor state of repair.

Third, one often meets the case where a partnership takes a lease of premises which have been allowed by the previous owner to get into a run-down state and the lease includes a covenant on the part of the partnership to reinstate the property in a good state of repair. In this sort of situation it is probable that, in spite of the Odeon decision, the Inland Revenue could successfully argue that the cost of carrying out the initial repairs was really part of the cost of obtaining the lease and it would therefore be capital and not allowable as a business expense. In practice, this third situation often arises in conjunction with a provision in the lease for rent to be waived for a period.

For example, a partnership might enter into premises under a lease which contained a covenant for the partnership to do initial repairs and in exchange for this the lease would provide that the partnership would pay no rent for, say, the first six months. If the Inland Revenue were then to argue (as they probably could) that the initial repairs were capital and not allowable, the partnership would have to face the unpleasant fact that it had exchanged a payment of tax-allowable rent for non-allowable initial repairs! A partnership faced with this common situation at the time of taking a lease of premises may well be much better off to arrange for the lessor to carry out the initial repairs and for the partnership to pay the rent in full.

Special Situations

So far in this chapter the three general rules for tax allowability of expenditure have been considered; we have been examining, in a general way, the first three questions set out at the beginning of the chapter with appropriate excursions into specific examples. It will be recalled, however, that there was a fourth question: expenditure can still be disallowed, even if it passes the three general tests, if it is specifically disallowed by the tax legislation. A common example of expenditure which is specifically disallowed by legislation is the cost of entertaining.

On the other hand, there are some items of expenditure which would fail to pass the three general tests but which, because of special favourable provisions in the tax legislation, are allowed or partly allowed against a partnership's profits.

A payment of a premium on a lease is an example of such an item of expenditure. The premium falls foul of the general tests: it is capital expenditure. It would seem, then, that it will not be allowed against profits but special rules in the tax legislation grant some allowance.

Entertaining expenses and lease premiums are just two examples of special situations, one on each side of the coin. There are a great many such special situations and the remaining paragraphs of this chapter include a review of the main rules relating to some selected items (including entertaining and lease premiums already touched upon) which do not conform to the three basic tests for tax allowability. There is also included a discussion of the tax treatment of some specific items of expenditure which do conform to the three basic tests but which, nevertheless, are worthy of brief specific discussion as they sometimes give rise to problems in the context of the taxation of partnership profits.

(To avoid misunderstanding on the part of readers, it should perhaps be mentioned that, in the interests of simplicity of presentation, the decision chart at the end of this chapter deliberately omits any reference to the relatively exceptional situation of expenditure which fails to pass the three tests but is nevertheless allowable because of special favourable provisions in the tax legislation.)

Entertaining Expenses and Gifts

The cost of entertaining business contacts passes the three basic tests; in particular, it is within the "wholly and exclusively" test since the cost is incurred with a business motive. But, nevertheless, expenditure on business entertainment is not, in general, an allowable deduction from a partnership's trading income because of specific statutory rules which disallow it.

There are, however, two major exceptions to the general rule prohibiting a deduction for business entertainment. Firstly, the cost of entertaining overseas customers (and the word "customers" can be read as "clients" in appropriate cases) is allowable. The recipient of the entertainment does not have to be a committed customer for the expenditure to be allowable; it is enough for him to be a potential customer in the sense that the partnership can reasonably expect him to become a customer in the future. But, as happens so often in tax matters, the overseas customer exemption is not quite as wide as it seems on a first reading. This is because of the way in which the tax legislation defines an overseas customer. Expressed very simply, an overseas customer or potential customer must be someone who is carrying on a *business* outside the United Kingdom. If, say, a firm of solicitors entertains a wealthy private individual (as distinct from a business executive) who lives in the United States and is one of their clients then the cost of this entertaining will, in strictness, *not* be allowed.

The second exception to the general rule prohibiting a deduction for entertaining relates to the cost of staff entertaining, such as staff outings and parties: this will be allowable. The authors' experience is that very many partnerships are unaware of this important practical point. The firm's annual staff Christmas beano can be quite lavish and will be allowed. As will a partnership silver jubilee banquet or something similar for staff members. But in one case known to the authors, a particularly Scrooge-like Inspector of Taxes argued that a firm that invited the wives of staff members to the office Christmas dinner-dance could obtain no allowance for the cost of entertaining the wives, as they were not themselves part of the firm's staff.

The word "entertaining" is very widely defined in the tax statutes and it includes the making of a gift. The cost of business gifts will therefore not be allowed against partnership profits (unless the recipients of the gifts are within the favoured classes of overseas customers or staff already referred to above). There is, though, a rather miserly exception which permits an allowance for the cost of providing gifts if the cost per recipient each year does not exceed £2 and the gift incorporates a conspicuous advertisement for the donor partnership. But to emphasise the fact that the Chancellor of the Exchequer frowns upon business "wining and dining" an advertising gift must not be drink, food or tobacco or the cost will be disallowed.

Lease Premiums

Where a partnership pays a premium for the grant of a lease of business premises for less than fifty years, tax legislation allows the partnership to deduct a proportion of the premium paid for business income. As was mentioned earlier under the heading "Special situations", this is an instance of a payment which would be disallowed completely but for a specific favourable provision in the tax legislation. No allowance is available where the lease is granted for fifty years or more.

Only a proportion of the premium paid is deductible and the exact method of calculation is best shown by an example, which is followed by an explanation of the rules.

Example 3.2
A partnership pays a premium of £10,000 for the grant of a 21 year lease.

Premium paid	£10,000
Non-allowable proportion: (21 – 1) x 2% of £10,000	4,000
Amount allowable over term of lease	£ 6,000

The partnership will be able to deduct the £6,000 in equal instalments over the 21 years of the lease; that is at the rate of £286 each year. No relief is available against business income for the balance of £4,000.

The Lease Premium Formula
The allowable amount of £6,000 in example 3.2 is derived from the statutory formula. This formula directs that part of the lease premium most be left out of account in deciding the tax-allowable figure. The fraction of the premium to be left out of account is:

$$(n - 1) \times 2\%,$$

where n is the number of complete years comprised in the duration of the lease. The result of this rather odd formula is that the shorter the period of the lease the greater will be the allowable portion of the premium, an important practical point.

Other Payments Under Leases

The explanation so far about leases had concentrated on the payment of lease premiums. In practice, though, one meets a wide variety of lump-sum payments made under leases which probably fall foul of one of the three basic tests but which are nevertheless allowable wholly or in part because of the specific favourable tax rules relating to payments under leases. Because of the practical importance of this subject it is worth expanding the previous discussion on lease premiums to cover some other types of lease lump-sum payments. The explanation of the law on the subject is best introduced by a practical case history.

Case History 3.3

Consider the fictional case of Lessee Associates, a hypothetical firm of architects. Lessee has a seven year lease on its office premises and the lease contains the usual option to renew for another seven years.

The option to renew is available to Lessee only if it has paid the rent and performed and observed all the covenants in the lease. Included among the lease covenants is the customary clause preventing Lessee from assigning or underletting the premises without the consent of the landlords. There is another covenant which prevents the premises being used for purposes other than those specified in the lease.

Lessee sublets part of its office premises without informing the landlords which is clearly in breach of the two covenants. Under provisions in the lease document, the lease is forfeited in the event of breach of covenant. On discovering the sub-letting, the landlords notify Lessee that they intend to forfeit the lease as a result of the breaches.

Negotiations then commence between Lessee and the landlords and ultimately it is agreed that Lessee makes a payment of £1,750 to the landlords in consideration of the landlords restoring the rights of Lessee to exercise the seven-year renewal option.

The imaginary partnership of Lessee Associates has made a lump-sum payment under a business lease amounting to £1,750. The payment is capital expenditure in the income tax sense and it therefore falls foul of one of the three basic tests. But can Lessee Associates make a claim for any part of the £1,750 against its business profits under the special tax rules relating to payments under leases? This question will now be considered.

Lease Payments – Some Practical Lessons

The most common situation where the (n – 1) x 2% formula applies is in connection with a payment made on the original grant of a lease; that is, an amount commonly called a premium. But the formula also applies to a number of payments that are likened to premiums by the tax legislation, particularly a payment made as consideration for varying or waiving a provision of the lease.

In the case history above the amount of £1,750 has been paid by Lessee Associates to the landlords in return for the landlords waiving the forfeiture provision in the lease. The result is that Lessee Associates will be entitled to set against its business profits part of the £1,750, using the (n – 1) x 2% formula. The tax relief that is available is not easily recognisable because of the complex legal rules surrounding it, and the simple practical message that emerges from all this is that any partnership that makes a lump-sum payment under a lease should carefully and expertly review the circumstances to see whether (as in the case of the fictional firm, Lessee Associates) the transaction fits within the tax-relieving provisions.

One final practical point on lease payments. What if your partnership pays a lump-sum not on the grant of a new lease but on acquiring the tail-end of an existing lease? For example, Tenant Ltd may have taken a 21-year lease from Landlord Ltd in March 1969. Suppose that in March 1979, your firm pays Tenant Ltd £10,000 to take over the remaining 11 years of the original lease. The payment of £10,000 is clearly capital but can your firm obtain any deduction from its business profits by using the (n – 1) x 2% formula or something similar? The answer to this question will be found to be almost unbelievable by those readers who are not yet convinced that tax and business commonsense are strangers to each other.

If your partnership pays £10,000 to Tenant Ltd, there may well be some tax allowance to your firm. But the allowance will not be based on the amount of £10,000; your firm will inherit from Tenant Ltd any tax deduction that they were obtaining for a lease premium on the particular premises and you will continue to obtain this deduction over the remaining period of the lease (assuming, of course, that you hold it until the end). The lesson here is clear and little known: when you acquire what is left of an existing lease you must discover from your predecessor whether he was entitled to any tax deduction from profits in respect of a lease premium and how much.

Redundancy Payments

It will be remembered from earlier discussion in this chapter (under the heading "Pre-business and post-business expenses") that expenses incurred by a partnership after it has ceased business will not be allowable as the expenses cannot strictly be said to be for the purposes of the business. In relation to redundancy payments, here is another instance of a specific favourable provision being inserted in the tax statutes to overrule the three basic tests. In general, all statutory redundancy payments are allowed for tax purposes.

Legal and Other Professional Expenses

The tax allowability of legal costs and other professional costs paid by a partnership sometimes causes problems in practice. This is an instance where the answer can generally be found by applying the three basic tests but nevertheless a few comments on this specific item of expenditure will probably be helpful to many partnerships and their advisers.

Legal and other professional costs in connection with the acquisition of a capital asset are themselves treated as capital expenditure and are therefore not allowable against profit, even if the expenditure proves abortive. If, therefore, a partnership engages a surveyor to advise on the proposed purchase of office premises and a solicitor to carry out legal searches there will be no deduction from profits for their charges even if the project is abandoned so that no capital asset is actually acquired. The gross inequity of this is apparent and calls for no further comment other than sympathy for the partnership concerned.

The same principle does, in strict law, apply if a firm uses its own internal estate and legal departments to carry out the work. But, in practice, the expenditure in these circumstances is normally allowed as a deduction from profits largely as a matter of convenience.

So far we have examined the professional costs relating to the acquisition or proposed acquisition of capital assets. If, however, costs are incurred not in acquiring additional assets but in maintaining or preserving existing assets then such expenditure will not be capital and will, in general, be allowed against profits. In the 1940 case of Southern v. Borax Consolidated Ltd the company held land in the United States on which it owned buildings. Legal action was taken in the States against the company requesting an order that the company had no legal title to the land and buildings. The company incurred legal costs in defending this action and subsequently the Inspector of Taxes argued that no deduction was due in respect of these costs as the expenditure was capital. The Courts rejected the Inspector's arguments and allowed the expenses on the grounds that they were not capital as they were incurred in an attempt to preserve ownership of an existing asset. A very useful principle to bear in mind in tax battles.

Salaries and Other Amounts Paid to Partners

Here is another instance where the tax treatment can be arrived at by considering the three basic tests but a deeper explanation seems nevertheless to be appropriate.

Partnerships commonly make payments of salaries and interest on capital to one or more of their partners. These payments are not within the "wholly and exclusively" test. They are made not for the purposes of the business but in determining how the business profit should be allocated. Therefore, salaries and interest on capital paid to partners will not be allowed as a deduction against profits but, on the other side of the coin, they will not be separately taxed as part of the income of the partners receiving them. In this respect, salaries and interest are treated in much the same way as partners' drawings, as was explained in chapter 1.

The discussion above about salaries relates to what are often called full partners. Many firms have salaried partners and it is beyond the scope of this guide to discuss in detail the contentious question as to the circumstances in which salaried partners are properly to be treated as partners for tax purposes. In practice, though, a large number of firms treat their salaried partners as no more than superior employees for tax purposes and this is generally acceptable to the Inland Revenue in most instances. If a salaried partner is treated as an employee rather than as a full partner then the salary paid to him will not be dealt with in the way described above but will be allowed as an expense along with other business salaries.

Returning now to the treatment of interest paid to partners on their capital, the rule is different if a partner receives interest not on his capital invested in the partnership but on some separate semi-permanent loan that he has made to the partnership. In this case, the interest paid will normally be allowed against profits as a partnership expense and, on the other-side of the coin, separately taxed in the hands of the partner receiving the interest. A similar result would normally follow if a partner charges the firm rent for the use of his personal property. But in both of these situations (that is, a partner making a long-term loan to the firm or letting a property to the firm) consideration ought to be given to the possibility of no payment or only a minimum reasonable payment being made as interest or rent. This is because the partner receiving the interest or rent will have it treated for tax as investment income which is, generally speaking, charged to income tax at a higher rate than his share of the firm's business profits.

If a partner makes a loan to his firm at a nil, or low, rate of interest, it should if possible be repayable on demand, otherwise there might be capital transfer tax liability. Similarly a letting to the firm at a nil, or low, rent should if possible be on a week-to-week or month-to-month basis, otherwise there might be capital transfer tax and capital gains tax liabilities.

Chapter 3 — Decision summary

The purpose of this chapter has been to outline a large area of partnership tax law, principally to enable a partner to form his own tentative decision on whether an item of expenditure is allowable or disallowable for tax purposes. To assist in reaching this decision, the general approach described in this chapter is summarised in compact form in the appended decision chart, which is placed after the tax mitigation check-list.

CHAPTER THREE

TAX MITIGATION CHECK-LIST

Taking new premises: don't have a covenant in the lease document compelling you to carry out "initial repair" work as a condition of being granted the lease.

Entertaining expenses: avoid the fairly common error of failing to claim a deduction for the cost of entertaining staff.

Business leases and lump-sum payments: remember that premium payments and many other types of lump-sums under leases qualify for some tax relief against profits — ensure that you make the claim.

Buying the tail of an existing lease: you must enquire of the vendor to see if you have inherited any tax deduction with the lease.

Rent and interest (on loans) paid to a partner: this is investment income in the hands of the recipient partner — there may be a tax saving if the financial arrangements are varied.

CHAPTER THREE

DECISION CHART FOR ALLOWABLE AND DISALLOWABLE EXPENDITURE

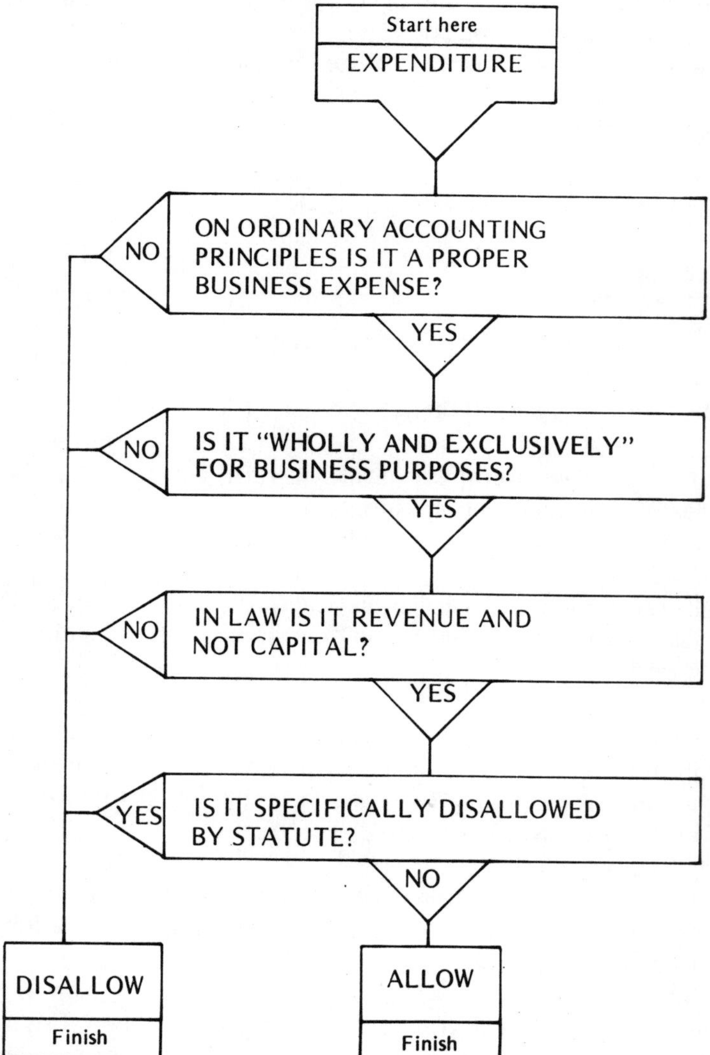

Note: This chart should be used as a general guide only

CHAPTER FOUR

HOW ACCOUNTING YEARS ARE CHANGED INTO INCOME TAX YEARS

Introducing the Strange World of April 5th

Look again at the outline in chapter 1 of the several stages in calculating the tax payable by the firm of Stan & Ollie. Stage 3 reveals a puzzling transformation: the accounting year ending 30 June 1977 has been converted to the year ending 5 April 1979.

This change is a central feature of all partnership business taxation. It happens because partnerships are not assessed to tax for their accounting years. In this respect, they differ enormously from limited companies. A limited company preparing a set of business accounts for the year ending 30 June 1977 will receive a tax assessment for that accounting year; the rates of tax charged in the assessment will be the company tax rates applicable for the year ending 30 June 1977. But a partnership is not permitted to approach its tax affairs in this simple and direct way.

A partnership is assessed to tax (regardless of the date to which it makes up its accounts) for an arbitrary year, the year ending 5 April. This arbitrary period will be referred to in this book as the "income tax year" although, technically speaking, its correct name is the "year of assessment" (and there are some who refer to it as the "fiscal year".) And so a partnership preparing accounts to 30 June 1977 will find that the income tax rules (shortly to be fully explained) require the profits of that year to be assessed to tax for the income tax year ending 5 April 1979.

Having transformed the year ending 30 June 1977 to the year ending 5 April 1979, the tax rules then treat the business profit from July 1976 to June 1977 just as if it had actually been earned in the year to 5 April 1979! This oddity has a number of strange consequences but, for present purposes, it is sufficient to point out that as a result the profit in the year ending June 1977 is charged to income tax at the tax rates applicable for the income tax year ending 5 April 1979. There is a striking contrast between the principle of this situation and the tax assessment on a limited company referred to earlier.

If, then, partnerships are always to be charged to income tax for income tax years there must obviously be some carefully laid down procedures for turning accounting years into income tax years. The purpose of this chapter is two-fold: first, to explain in detail what these procedures are; second, to demonstrate as clearly as possible just what their practical effect is. This second aspect of the discussion is vitally important because the effect of the rules that we are now about to consider is cometimes freakish, and expert planning is often called for to avoid the pitfalls this creates and to maximise the opportunities.

Brief reference has already been made in this introduction to the rules regarding limited companies; the method of assessing companies is expanded upon in chapter 11. A change in the partners in a firm has an important bearing on the way in which accounting years are turned into income tax years and this is dealt with in chapter 5. The discussion in this chapter and in chapter 5 is solely concerned with the taxing of what might be termed business profits of a partnership. The discussion has no application to the assessment of extraneous items received by a partnership, for example, rent on partnership properties which are held as investments, interest received and partnership capital gains. In regard to all of these items special rules exist which are outside the scope of this particular book.

The Income Tax Year Written in Shorthand

Throughout this chapter and the succeeding chapters it will be necessary to make frequent references to the income tax year ending 5 April. It is very widely known that this is usually abbreviated so that, for example, the year ending 5 April 1979 is expressed as 1978/79. In general, this book will use the abbreviated form.

Tax Depreciation Allowances

An important digression is called for at this stage; for reasons which will become clear later, tax depreciation allowances need special mention before the explanations in this chapter can be proceeded with.

In chapters 6 and 7, the calculation of tax depreciation allowances (usually known as capital allowances) will be fully examined and we shall then see that the method of calculating capital allowances for income tax differs very substantially from the conventions usually adopted by accountants in calculating depreciation for accounting purposes. Two features of the capital allowances system need to be mentioned now, in advance of the fuller treatment in chapters 6 and 7. Firstly, the relatively simple and perhaps obvious point that in handling the calculations of a partnership's tax bill for any particular year it is necessary to eliminate from the partnership accounts the depreciation that has been charged according to accounting conventions and to substitute the different figure of capital allowances calculated according to tax rules.

Second, and a little more difficult to grasp, partnership capital allowances are always calculated in terms of income tax years. There is no such thing as capital allowances granted to a firm for the year ending 30 June 1977, for example. The capital allowances will be described as being for the year 1978/79 but they will be calculated by looking at the firm's capital assets (office machinery, etc) as they were in the year ending 30 June 1977.

An example will help to explain these two features of the capital allowances system. Suppose that for the year ending 30 June 1977 the partnership profit and loss account shows a profit of £40,000 after charging depreciation of assets amounting to £6,000. (For simplicity of understanding, let us make the assumption that there are no adjustments to be made to the partnership profit before it becomes acceptable for tax purposes, other than the figure of depreciation.) The amount of £6,000 will be eliminated as an expense against profits for tax purposes thus increasing the taxable profit for the year ending 30 June 1977 to £46,000. This profit of £46,000 for an accounting year is now converted to an income tax assessment for an income tax year, *before* deducting capital allowances. The year ending 30 June 1977 becomes 1978/79 (precisely how will be explained in this chapter) and the assessment for the income tax year 1978/79, before capital allowances are deducted, is £46,000. Capital allowances are then calculated for the income tax year 1978/79. Although the calculations will be made by looking at the firm's capital assets in the year ending 30 June 1977 the answer is most unlikely to be the figure of £6,000 depreciation charged in the partnership profit and loss account for that year because (as chapters 6 and 7 will explain) the tax rules for calculating depreciation differ substantially from the conventions usually adopted in preparing business accounts. Suppose that the amount of the capital allowances for 1978/79 is £8,000. The result is that the income tax assessment on the partnership for the year 1978/79 is a profit of £46,000 less capital allowances of £8,000 giving a net assessment of £38,000. It is on this amount of £38,000 that the firm's income tax bill will be calculated for 1978/79.

Of course, precisely the same practical result would have been achieved if the capital allowances of £8,000 had been deducted from the profit of £46,000 *before* the year ending 30 June 1977 was turned into the income tax year 1978/79. The reader is therefore forgiven if he concludes that this explanation is nothing more than technical gobbledegook producing a distinction without a difference. But there are some instances (one will be explained towards the end of this chapter) where the difference is a real and important one.

This explanation in advance of the chapters devoted to capital allowances has had to go into a fair amount of detail; why was it necessary at this stage? Primarily, to establish clearly the background of the figures used in the discussion in this chapter and the next. Whenever profit figures are used in these two chapters, the amounts given are the business profits as adjusted for income tax purposes. In particular, this means the profit as it would have been if no depreciation had been charged in the business accounts; the profit figures given in the following discussions are the equivalent of the £46,000 in the example above. And whenever, in this and the next chapter, profit figures for an accounting year have been turned into tax assessments for an income tax year, the reader must understand that, in practice, a deduction for capital allowances will be given.

The authors are aware that many readers, having digested all that has been said above, will still feel that, on the subject of partnership capital allowances, the tax laws seem to have produced a situation comparable to using differential calculus to show that 2 + 2 = 4. They ask those particular readers to be patient; the full significance of this round-about journey through the subject will, hopefully, become apparent as this chapter proceeds.

Relating Accounting Years to Income Tax Years

Now to the meat of this chapter. Probably the easiest way to understand the principles involved in converting accounting years to income tax years is, first, to put yourself in the place of the Inland Revenue authorities when, very many years ago, they were faced with the daunting task of devising a workable solution to the problem. Many possible approaches must have presented themselves — let us consider some of them so that we may lead easily to the method that was actually adopted.

For the purposes of this explanation, consider a partnership preparing accounts each year to 30 June. A time span of about four years or so in the life of the partnership could be set out in the form of a strip diagram in which one strip shows the firm's accounting years and the other shows the income tax years:

1.7.76 to 30.6.77	1.7.77 to 30.6.78	1.7.78 to 30.6.79	1.7.79 to 30.6.80

6.4.76 to 5.4.77	6.4.77 to 5.4.78	6.4.78 to 5.4.79	6.4.79 to 5.4.80

In the diagram the upper strip shows the accounting years and the lower strip shows the income tax years; they are placed approximately in corresponding positions to each other in terms of the calendar.

Let us now concentrate our attention on a representative accounts year: the accounts year from 1 July 1977 to 30 June 1978. Consider some of the choices that were available to the Inland Revenue authorities when they were devising the rules on how this accounts year should be turned into an income tax year.

They could have done this:

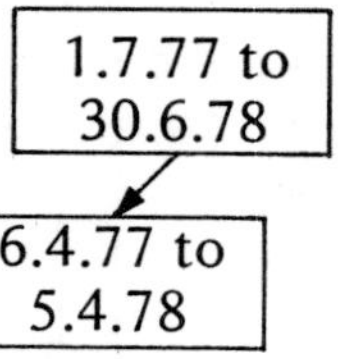

That is, the tax statutes could have directed that the year ending 30 June 1978 be converted into the income tax year 1977/78 because these two years corresponded most closely to each other in the calendar sense. A logical approach which would probably have commended itself to many businessmen – it was not adopted.

Or the tax statutes could have turned the year ending 30 June 1978 to an income tax year in the following way:

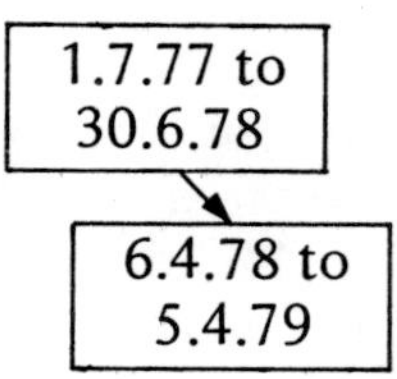

It could have been laid down that the year ending 30 June was to be converted to the income tax year 1978/79 because the closing date of the accounts year (30 June 1978) falls inside the income tax year 1978/79. Another reasonably sensible approach to the problem – again, not adopted.

Neither of these two straightforward solutions was used by the Inland Revenue authorities when the present rules were devised some fifty years ago. The correct answer is that the year ending 30 June 1978 will be transformed into the income tax year 1979/80:

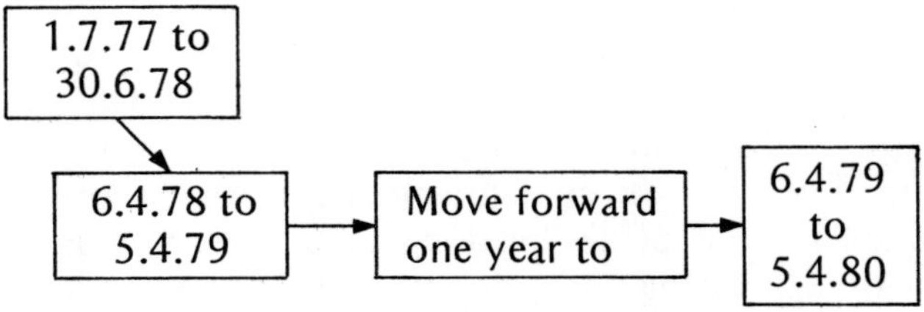

The rule then in normal circumstances (some variations will be dealt with later in this chapter) for converting an accounts year to an income tax year can be expressed in two stages:

1. Take the closing date of the accounts year and find in what income tax year it falls.
2. Move forward one year to the next income tax year. This is the answer.

Going back now to the hypothetical firm of Stan & Ollie referred to in chapter 1 we can see how the year ending 30 June 1977 has been transformed to the year 1978/79: the date 30 June 1977 falls in the income tax year 1977/78 and we have moved forward one year from this to 1978/79.

Some other examples, taking dates at random, are:

The profit earned in the accounting year ending 31 March 1978 will be assessed to income tax for the income tax year 1978/79

The profit earned in the accounting year ending 30 April 1978 will be assessed to income tax for the income tax year 1979/80

The profit earned in the accounting year ending 31 January 1979 will be assessed to income tax for the income tax year 1979/80

This accounts year/tax year relationship can also be approached in the reverse way; that is, how to take an income tax year and turn it back into an accounts year. In this form, the rule is rather more complex to state but, with the help of the last diagram above, readers should be able to answer this question: if you are looking at your firm's tax assessment for any particular income tax year how do you discover the accounts year on which it is based? The answer, of course, is that you move backwards one year to the preceding income tax year and you then find the accounts year that ended in that preceding income tax year. This reverse method of expressing the rule is admittedly more complex but it is set out here for one reason in particular. This tortuous approach, rather than the simpler method adopted earlier, is the form of words used in the tax statute – predictably enough, some will say. Because of this, the method of relating accounts years to income tax years that has just been fully explained is almost always referred to as the *preceding-year basis* of assessment. (Often shortened, by those who wish to demonstrate that they have been initiated into the subject, to the p.y. basis).

The Early Years of a New Partnership

The preceding-year basis is unsuitable in the early years of a new partnership (and, as we shall see later, in the closing years of a partnership). For example, if a new partnership commences in the income tax year 1978/79 it will expect to be taxed for the first time (and indeed will be taxed for the first time) for that income tax year, that is 1978/79. The preceding-year basis obviously cannot apply in assessing the partnership for 1978/79 since the partnership did not exist before 1978/79.

This particular problem – the first of the variations from the normal preceding-year rule that we are about to review – was not beyond the wit and intelligence of the inventor of the partnership tax assessment rules. He decided (quite rightly) that special rules were needed for the first two income tax years of a partnership's existence. After that the preceding-year basis could be operated in the normal way. What then are the procedures to be adopted in income tax years 1 and 2?

Income Tax Year 1

Suppose that a new partnership business commences on 1 October 1978. The first income tax year for which this partnership will be liable to tax will be 1978/79 and the rule is that the income tax assessment for that year will be the amount of profits made from 1 October 1978 to 5 April 1979.

Now readers are going to raise mental objections to the fact that this new partnership will have to prepare a set of accounts at such an inconvenient date as 5 April 1979. In fact, it will not be required to do this. It is more than likely that the new partnership will prepare its first business accounts to 30 September 1979, and the profit for the period from 1 October 1978 to 5 April 1979 will be calculated by taking a simple time proportion of twelve-months profits. If the accounts for the first year ending 30 September 1979 show a profit as adjusted for tax purposes of £16,000, then the income tax assessment on the partnership for 1978/79 will be a little over a six-months' proportion of this figure or, in simple round figures, £8,000.

The rule then for the first income tax year of a new partnership is that it is assessed to tax on the profit it makes from the date of its commencement until the following 5 April. Another way of expressing this rule is to say that for the first income tax year the amount assessed to tax is the profits actually earned in the income tax year itself. Because of this, the rule is often referred to in practice as the "actual profits" basis but as this phrase tends to be understood only by those who are familiar with the subject the phrase "profits earned in the income tax year" will be used generally in this book.

Income Tax Year 2

The rule for the second income tax year is relatively simple to state but difficult to justify by any arithmetical logic.

For the second income tax year of a new partnership business, the tax assessment will be the profits that have been earned in the first twelve months of business activity. Returning to the example above of a partnership business commencing on 1 October 1978, the second income tax year will be 1979/80 and the assessment for this year will be the amount of business profits for the year ending 30 September 1979. Using the figure above, the 1979/80 assessment will be £16,000.

Income Tax Year 3 and Subsequent Years

All is now plain sailing. The partnership will be able to operate the preceding-year basis. (For completeness, it should be mentioned that problems may arise in calculating the assessment for income tax year 3 if the first set of accounts prepared for the business is for an abnormal period of time, say for 9 months or 15 months. The Inland Revenue have adopted certain standard practices in this type of situation but these are outside the scope of the discussion in this practical guide to the subject.)

The precise practical effect of the explanation so far can best be understood by an example.

Example 4.1

John Novice and Partners open up a new estate agency business on 1 July 1978. The business profits for the first few years (as adjusted for income tax purposes) are as follows:-

Year ending 30 June 1979	£6,000
Year ending 30 June 1980	8,000
Year ending 30 June 1981	20,000
Year ending 30 June 1982	25,000
and so on.	

The first income tax assessment on this partnership will be for 1978/79 and the assessments for all years will be as follows:-

1978/79	Profit earned in the income tax year (9 months and 5 days)	say	£4,500
79/80	Profits for first 12 months		6,000
80/81	Preceding-year basis		6,000
81/82	Preceding-year basis		8,000
82/83	Preceding-year basis		20,000
83/84	Preceding-year basis		25,000
and so on.			

(To avoid doubt in the mind of the reader, it is confirmed that most of the above income tax assessments for the six years shown will be reduced by capital allowances as explained above under the heading "Tax depreciation allowances". Similarly with regard to the subsequent examples in this chapter.)

Multiplication of Profits

The example clearly demonstrates an important consequence of the rules relating to the taxation of a new partnership business: the profits of a particular period are used to measure the amount of tax payable more than once. The profits for the year ended 30 June 1979 are brought into the tax assessment calculations 2¾ times! This multiplication of profits will always happen but, as we shall see later in this chapter, there is some compensation to the partnership at a subsequent time.

What if Profits Fall Away?

The multiplication of the first year's profits is, perhaps, acceptable if, as in the case of John Novice & Partners, the profits are on a rising graph. After all, the first year's profits of £6,000 are being used to measure the tax payable for the income tax year 1980/81, by which time the profits are running at a much higher level. Most readers will agree that this is no bad thing.

But John Novice & Partners would be less happy if for the income tax year 1980/81 they were being taxed on the first year's profits but business had fallen away so that in the years ending 30 June 1980 and 30 June 1981 they were making much less than £6,000. With a sweet reasonableness that is wholly untypical of taxing law, the statutes make provision for just this possibility.

If it suits a new partnership to do so, it may abandon the rules for calculating the tax assessment for income tax years 2 and 3: in the above example the years 1979/80 and 1980/81. At its option, the partnership may calculate its assessments for these two tax years as the amount of the profits actually earned by it in each of the two income tax years.

This is entirely a one-way option: the Inland Revenue cannot alter the assessments for tax years 2 and 3 to the profits actually earned in order to produce a higher tax liability. Only the partnership is given this option and, of course, it will only use it if it produces a lower figure of tax. But the partnership cannot pick and choose between years 2 and 3. It must either use the basis shown in example 4.1 for *both* years 2 and 3 or it must choose to be assessed on the profits actually earned for *both* years 2 and 3. In broad terms, this important option protects a firm, whose profits fall away after the first year or so, from serious tax disadvantage.

What is Meant by a New Partnership?

In example 4.1, John Novice & Partners started a totally new activity from nothing. But, apart from this obvious instance, a new partnership business is regarded for tax purposes as having commenced whenever there is a change in the partners themselves. If John Novice & Partners had been established for very many years past with, say, six partners and on 1 July 1978 a seventh partner was added then this would bring into operation the early-years rules as shown in example 4.1. The partnership may, however, opt out of these rules if it wishes; this is dealt with fully in the next chapter.

The Closing Years of a Partnership Business

Now to the other end of the partnership's life scale. Suppose, to take a simple case, that a partnership business which has always prepared its accounts to 31 December closes down completely on 31 December 1978. In the ordinary course of events, using the preceding-year basis, the accounts for the last year ending 31 December 1978 would have been used as the basis for taxing the partnership for the income tax year 1979/80. But, since the business closed down in 1978/79 (on 31 December 1978), do the Inland Revenue have the power to make an income tax assessment for the subsequent year 1979/80? The answer is no.

There is a fundamental principle of tax law which prevents assessments being made for any income tax year which falls after the time when the business closed. As a result, the last income tax assessment that can be made on the partnership is for the income tax year 1978/79. And so in the closing years of a partnership business we have a set of rules which can be considered to be the converse of the rules in the early years: in the early years it takes some time before the preceding-year basis begins to operate and in the closing years the preceding-year basis is phased out.

Before explaining the way in which this is done it is worth repeating (from a different angle) the point made above under the heading "What is meant by a new partnership?"

A partnership business will be treated as having closed down when there is a change in the partners. John Novice & Partners, a few paragraphs back, took in a seventh partner on 1 July 1978; it was treated as having commenced a new partnership business. But equally the previous partnership is regarded as having closed. Again, this is subject to the options which will be explained in the next chapter. The treatment of a partnership change as a closure and an opening of a new business makes the rules that are now about to be explained and the treatment of the early years already discussed of considerable practical importance.

Reverting to the example of the partnership business that closes down on 31 December 1978, the rules that we are now about to discuss relate to the income tax assessments for the income tax years (going backwards in time) 1978/79, 1977/78 and 1976/77. No other years are affected by the special rules; earlier years will have been taxed on the preceding-year basis and will remain as they are. These three years are often referred to by the titles: ultimate year, penultimate year and ante-penultimate year. To avoid these fearsome descriptions the explanation that follows refers to the income tax year in which the partnership closes as the closing tax year, and the two prior tax years are referred to as closing tax year minus 1 (CTY – 1) and closing tax year minus 2 (CTY – 2).

Example 4.2

The Peter Out Partnership which has been established for many years, preparing accounts each year to 30 June, closes down on 30 June 1980. (Of course, partnerships will not necessarily close down on their accounting date in practice. The principles about to be discussed apply regardless of the date of closure but the arithmetic is simpler to understand if the accounting date is taken as the closing date.) The profits (adjusted for tax purposes) for the final accounting year and for a recent run of years are as follows:-

Year ending 30 June 1980	£10,000
Year ending 30 June 1979	8,000
Year ending 30 June 1978	16,000
Year ending 30 June 1977	12,000
Year ending 30 June 1976	18,000

and so on.

The income tax assessments based on these facts are considered in the succeeding paragraphs.

Closing Tax Year

The closing tax year in example 4.2 is 1980/81 and (as already explained) it is necessary to review the income tax assessments for 1980/81, 1979/80 and 1978/79. It eases understanding if these years are considered going backwards in time.

For 1980/81, The Peter Out Partnership may possibly already have received from its Inspector of Taxes an income tax demand calculated on a preceding-year basis; that is, an amount of £8,000 based on the year ending 30 June 1979. If so, the demand based on the preceding-year will be completely scrapped. In its place, the tax rules require that the partnership be assessed on the basis of the profits earned in the income tax year 1980/81. The assessment will therefore be on a time proportion covering the period from 6 April 1980 to 30 June 1980, a little under three months. As near enough as matters, the 1980/81 assessment will be £2,500, three-twelfths of £10,000.

The rule is that for the closing tax year a partnership will be assessed to tax on the profits actually earned in the income tax year itself (commonly referred to as the actual profits basis).

CTY – 1 and CTY – 2

It is necessary to consider these two years taken together. Returning to the facts used in example 4.2 for The Peter Out Partnership, the income tax assessments for these two years will already have been dealt with on the preceding-year basis as follows:-

1979/80 assessment: year ending 30 June 1978	£16,000
1978/79 assessment: year ending 30 June 1977	12,000

An interesting (dare one say, exciting?) feature now emerges if we review the tax assessments on The Peter Out Partnership for the three years 1978/79, 1979/80 and 1980/81. It will be seen that a considerable time period never enters into the calculation of the income tax assessments.

The profit made by the firm during the period from 1 July 1978 to 5 April 1980 does not form part of any income tax assessment. Many business partners find it difficult to believe that this can be so but it is an essential feature of the system of taxing partnership profits; it is, as some readers will have already recognised, the natural converse of the multiplication of profits in the early years.

This period of time which is effectively by-passed for tax purposes will need to be referred to in the important discussion that follows and it is convenient to give it a title. There is no official phrase available to describe it (not surprisingly, since at the official level there is little desire to talk about it) but in this book it will be referred to as "the pass-over period"; this is an apt description and the Biblical analogy with those who were spared by the destroying angel is not altogether inappropriate to income tax.

The pass-over period can, in some way, be regarded as fair compensation for the multiplication of profits in the early years of a partnership business. Remarkable though it may be, the Inland Revenue are, therefore, prepared to accept it as part of the system of taxing partnership profits. But they are concerned that the dice would be loaded against them if the pass-over period happened to be a time of exceptionally high profits, or if a partnership with astute advisers deliberately engineered a richly profitable pass-over period. In an attempt to defend them against such a situation, the Inland Revenue have been given powers in the tax statutes to alter the tax assessments on a partnership for the closing tax year minus 1 and the closing tax year minus 2. These two years will have been assessed on the preceding-year basis and the Inland Revenue may eliminate this basis and substitute for both of these years tax assessments equal to the profits earned in the income tax years. Before we consider the figure work involved in this, let us examine the practical effect.

If, in the case of The Peter Out Partnership, the Inland Revenue were to alter the assessments for CTY — 1 and CTY — 2 the result would be as follows:-

1979/80 assessment : profits from 6 April 1979 to 5 April 1980

1978/79 assessment : profits from 6 April 1978 to 5 April 1979

This power given to the Inland Revenue to alter the assessments if it suits them does not go back further than the two years: the 1977/78 assessment must remain on the preceding-year basis, on the profits for the year ending 30 June 1976. What have the Inland Revenue achieved? The pass-over period has not been eliminated, all that has happened is that it has moved.

As was demonstrated earlier, if the preceding-year basis applies for 1978/79 and 1979/80, the pass-over period runs from 1 July 1978 to 5 April 1980. And, if the Inland Revenue use their rights to alter the assessments for 1978/79 and 1979/80, the pass-over period is still there and is still of the same duration but it is in a different place: from 1 July 1976 to 5 April 1978. That, then, is the important practical effect of the closing years rules. Now to complete the arithmetic of example 4.2.

Example 4.2 continued

We have already seen under the heading "Closing tax year" above that the income tax assessment on The Peter Out Partnership for 1980/81 will be £2,500. For 1979/80 and 1978/79 the Inland Revenue will choose between the two alternative approaches available to them.

First, the preceding-year basis:-

1979/80 : profits of year ending 30 June 1978	£16,000
1978/79 : profits of year ending 30 June 1977	12,000
	£28,000

Second, the profits earned in the two income tax years (the actual profits basis). The calculation in months, ignoring small fractions of a month, are:-

1979/80 :	3/12 of 8,000	2,000	
	9/12 of 10,000	7,500	£9,500
1978/79 :	3/12 of 16,000	4,000	
	9/12 of 8,000	6,000	10,000
			£19,500

The Inland Revenue have the choice. The partnership has no option in the matter at all. Clearly, the Inland Revenue will choose the basis that produces the higher assessments: 1979/80 and 1978/79 will therefore remain on the preceding-year basis.

The income tax assessments on The Peter Out Partnership can now be finally listed as follows:-

1980/81	£ 2,500
1979/80	16,000
1978/79	12,000
1977/78	18,000
and so on.	

Example 4.2 modified
To demonstrate beyond any doubt the precise effect of the Inland Revenue powers for closing tax year minus 1 and closing tax year minus 2, consider The Peter Out Partnership again but with the figures slightly modified:-

Year ending 30 June 1980	£10,000
Year ending 30 June 1979	16,000
Year ending 30 June 1978	12,000
Year ending 30 June 1977	8,000
Year ending 30 June 1976	18,000
and so on.	

As before, the income tax assessment for the closing tax year 1980/81 will be £2,500. Now consider the Inland Revenue powers for the years 1979/80 and 1978/79.

First, on the preceding-year basis the tax assessments would be:-

1979/80 : profits of year ending 30 June 1978	£12,000
1978/79 : profits of year ending 30 June 1977	8,000
	£20,000

Second, on the alternative basis of profits earned in the two income tax years:-

1979/80 : 3/12 of 16,000	4,000	
9/12 of 10,000	7,500	£11,500
1978/79 : 3/12 of 12,000	3,000	
9/12 of 16,000	12,000	15,000
		£26,500

The arithmetic here is interesting since, if one compares the results of the two different methods, for one income tax year the assessment is higher and for the other it is lower. The Inland Revenue would like to be able to pick and choose in this type of situation but the tax statutes give them no such power. They must take one basis or the other for *both* years. By taking the profit earned in the income tax years rather than the preceding-year basis, the *total* tax assessments for the two years are higher and this will be the basis they will select.

The income tax assessments for all years will finally be as follows:-

1980/81	£ 2,500
1979/80	11,500
1978/79	15,000
1977/78	18,000

and so on.

CTY–1 and CTY–2 in a Nutshell

Summarising the discussion above, the rule is that the Inland Revenue are given the choice for these two years. Either the income tax assessments for *both* years will stay on the preceding-year basis, or *both* years will be assessed to income tax on the profits earned in the respective income tax years (the actual profits basis). But whichever basis is adopted by the Inland Revenue the result must be a pass-over period – a period of profits that will never be taken into account in calculating income tax assessments. The length of the pass-over period will vary from one case to another according to the normal accounting date adopted by the partnership.

The Overall Effect of the Early Years' and Closing Years' Rules

Having completed our journey through this remarkable labyrinth of technical rules, let us try to evaluate their overall practical effect.

The impact of the rules can be fully understood only by considering the income tax assessments on a partnership over its total life and this will be done shortly in the form of a practical case history. One thing though should be abundantly clear at this stage: over the entire life of a partnership business it would be a remarkable coincidence if the total income tax assessments equalled the total profits! Depending upon the pattern of profits, the business will pay tax on either more or less than it has actually earned.

Case History 4.3

In 1972, a fictional three-partner firm of architects, Wye Zed & Partners, had the opportunity of becoming involved in a new development project which was likely to run for a period of four or five years. Because the project required a specialist design skill, Wye Zed & Partners decided to bring into the project the part-time services of an architect from another practice with experience in the particular area. To conduct the project, a new additional partnership was formed called Wye Zed Associates with four partners: the three partners of Wye Zed & Partners and the outside specialist. Wye Zed & Partners continued separately with its three partners precisely as before. Wye Zed Associates was a new separate activity so that the early years' tax rules came into operation.

Wye Zed Associates commenced business on 1 July 1972. For the first three years or so the project was active and was producing income for Wye Zed Associates but by the fourth year the project had begun to run down and on 30 June 1977 Wye Zed Associates was brought to an end, it having completed the purpose for which it was created. The Wye Zed Associates business was completely closed down and dissolved so that the closing years' tax rules applied.

The profit record from the commencement of Wye Zed Associates to its end was as follows (the profits being, of course, the figures as adjusted for tax purposes):-

Year ending 30 June 1973	£10,000
Year ending 30 June 1974	12,000
Year ending 30 June 1975	13,200
Year ending 30 June 1976	120
Year ending 30 June 1977	300
Total profits	£35,620

The first income tax year for which Wye Zed Associates would be assessed to tax is 1972/73 (the business commenced in July 1972) and the closing income tax year is 1977/78. The partnership will therefore be assessed to tax for six income tax years altogether and the assessments are as follows:-

1972/73	profits earned in the income tax year, that is from 1 July 1972 to 5 April 1973 say	£7,500
1973/74	profits for the first twelve months of business	10,000
1974/75	preceding-year basis	10,000
1975/76	preceding-year basis	12,000
1976/77	preceding-year basis	13,200
1977/78	profits earned in the income tax year, that is 6 April 1977 to 30 June 1977 say	75
Total income tax assessments		£52,775

(The Inland Revenue have the right to alter the assessments for the two income tax years 1975/76 and 1976/77 from the preceding-year basis to the amounts of profits actually earned in each of these two tax years. An arithmetical calculation will show that the actual profits basis produces income tax assessments which are very much lower than the preceding-year basis. The Inland Revenue will, of course, not exercise their right to alter the assessments for these two years.)

A Cautionary Tale

The results shown in the case history can only be described as horrific. Wye Zed Associates have made total profits of £35,620 over the life of the partnership and have been assessed to income tax on £52,775. The four partners of Wye Zed Associates all have income from their other architectural firms and therefore it is likely that they are paying high rates of income tax. It would not be impossible for their tax rates to be such that the total income tax on £52,775 would be as high as, say, £38,000. It could well be that the total income tax on £52,775 actually amounts to more than the total profits made by the firm! And there is absolutely nothing that can be done under the tax statutes to cure this gross inequity.

The only alternative approach available to Wye Zed Associates was that described in this chapter under the heading "What if profits fall away?" when it was explained that for income tax year 2 and income tax year 3 (in this case, 1973/74 and 1974/75) the income tax assessments could be altered, at the option of the firm, to the amount of profits actually made in these two income tax years. But a quick arithmetical check will show that if Wye Zed Associates applies to exercise this option the income tax assessments for 1973/74 and 1974/75 will be higher than they are at present and the position will be worsened for them. This is not surprising since the firm's profits did not, in fact, fall away in the very early years.

What has caused this awful result from which there is no legal escape? It is the operation of, on the one hand, the multiplication of profits in the early years of business and, on the other, the pass-over period (to use the phrase that was introduced earlier in this chapter) in the closing years. As has already been explained, there will always be a multiplication period and a pass-over period in a partnership that commences and then closes. In the case of Wye Zed Associates the profits that have entered the multiplication period are very much higher than the profits bypassed in the pass-over period. The pattern of profits over the five accounting years could hardly have been worse from this point of view.

The practical lesson, of course, is to try to avoid a business situation that will produce the type of profit pattern shown in case history 4.3. Indeed, there are a number of profit patterns that will produce the attractive result of total income tax assessments which are considerably *less* than the total profits. Consider, for example, what the result would have been if the profits of Wye Zed Associates for the year ended 30 June 1973 and the year ended 30 June 1976 were transposed.

Case History 4.3 modified

Wye Zed Associates, which commenced business on 1 July 1972 and closed down on 30 June 1977, made the following profits:-

Year ending 30 June 1973	£ 120
Year ending 30 June 1974	12,000
Year ending 30 June 1975	13,200
Year ending 30 June 1976	10,000
Year ending 30 June 1977	300
Total profits	£35,620

The income tax assessments are:-

1972/73	profits earned in the income tax year, that is 1 July 1972 to 5 April 1973, say £	90
1973/74	profits for the first twelve months of business	120
1974/75	preceding-year basis	120
1975/76	preceding-year basis	12,000
1976/77	preceding-year basis	13,200
1977/78	profits earned in the income tax year, that is 6 April 1977 to 30 June 1977, say	75
	Total income tax assessments	£25,605

As in the original version of the case history, the Inland Revenue will not exercise their option to alter the assessments for 1975/76 and 1976/77, since this would reduce the income tax assessments. And the partnership would not exercise its option to alter 1973/74 and 1974/75 since this would increase the income tax assessments.

A Separate Partnership: A Tax Saving? — Or A Tax Trap?
The modified case history shows a substantial income tax reduction. Compared with the position had the five years' profits of Wye Zed Associates formed part of the profits of Wye Zed & Partners, a saving is generated; this saving does not appear in the early years of Wye Zed Associates (in fact, in the early years there is a very slight tax disadvantage compared with the position had the profit been made by Wye Zed & Partners) but it emerges at the time of closing the separate partnership. The existence of a separate partnership will create tax saving opportunities — and tax pitfalls for the unwary. The subject is one which, in practice, usually requires attention from tax practitioners experienced in the field of partnership planning, since one of the keys is the adoption of a correct pattern of profits.

The tax saving in the modified case history results from the particular pattern of profits. The case history is, in fact, a grossly simplified adaptation of a case with which one of the authors was involved in practice and it is included to demonstrate what can actually be done in a separate partnership. There are a number of profit patterns that will produce the beneficial result shown in the modified case history (including patterns which produce a considerably higher tax saving than that shown above). Equally, there are a number of profit patterns to be avoided since they produce the result shown in the original Wye Zed Associates case history. It is not possible to develop here, as fully as one would like, the discussion of what is the most favourable profit pattern, partly because this can be dependent upon individual factors, such as the partnership's accounting date. But returning for a moment to the discussion earlier in this chapter under the heading "Tax depreciation allowances", readers may now be able to discern a situation where a real and important significance attaches to the fact that capital allowances are deducted from tax assessments *after* accounts years have been changed into income tax years: capital allowance deductions cannot assist a partnership in attaining a desirable profit pattern or in avoiding an unfavourable one.

What of the Future?

Having explained all this, we have to tell you that there is talk of a change in the law. The Inland Revenue are aware that certain people have been engineering favourable profit patterns and they are considering scrapping the preceding-year basis of assessment altogether and switching to an actual profits basis for all years. However they have emphasised that their work is at a very early stage and this switch may not be practicable at all.

This has got to be borne in mind by anyone who is contemplating setting up a separate partnership. It seems almost certain that if this switch does take place it will not take place for some time; on the other hand it is only when a separate partnership has run for some years that it starts to achieve its tax savings. The message, we think, is that if readers do set up a separate partnership, then even if there is a change in the law before savings are achieved they will only be very slightly worse off than if they had done nothing, whereas if they do nothing they are missing the chance of making substantial savings.

To sum up

The creation of maximum tax savings from separate partnerships and the legal implementation of a sophisticated partnership plan are large subjects on which the bigger firms will usually need to take top-level tax advice. But the authors hope that what they have said will provide some practical assistance in setting guidelines for partners and their advisers in small and simple partnership cases.

Chapter 4 – The Rules Summarised

Taking the normal example of a partnership that prepares its business accounts for regular twelve-monthly time intervals, the income tax assessments will be based on the profits earned in the periods shown below:

–	Income tax year 1	From date of commencement to following 5 April (actual profits basis)
–	Income tax year 2	First twelve months of business – but see note A
–	Income tax year 3	Accounts year ending in the preceding income tax year (preceding-year basis) – but see note A *Note A* : The partnership (not the Inland Revenue) has the option to base both years 2 and 3 on the actual profits earned in those two years – *both* years, it should be noticed, not just one
–	Income tax year 4 and subsequently	Accounts year ending in the preceding income tax year (preceding-year basis) – this basis will continue to apply until the closing years' rules are reached.
–	Closing tax year minus 2	Preceding-year basis – but see note B
–	Closing tax year minus 1	Preceding-year basis – but see note B *Note B* : The Inland Revenue (not the partnership) has the option to base both CTY–2 and CTY–1 on the actual profits earned in those two years – *both* years, it should be noticed, not just one
–	Closing tax year	From 6 April prior to closure to date of closure (actual profits basis)

CHAPTER FOUR

TAX MITIGATION CHECK-LIST

In the early and closing years of a partnership, "monitor" the profit so that (so far as is commercially and legally possible) the business is conducted in a way that produces a desirable profit pattern rather than one with unfavourable tax consequences.

Consider the creation of legally separated short-term partnerships with tax-advantageous profit patterns.

Do nót overlook the options given to a partnership in income tax years 2 and 3. (Especially useful where a separate partnership has been created and the profit generated in the first year of business produces unfavourable tax consequences in income tax years 2 and 3.) There's plenty of time in which to formally exercise the option so there is no excuse for overlooking it! – you are permitted to claim it up until the end of income tax year 9 (yes, *nine*).

CHAPTER FIVE

CHANGING PARTNERS – THE INCOME TAX CONSEQUENCES

Introduction

During the life of a partnership, partners will come and go with a frequency which is usually determined by the size of the firm. Each such change in the partners has income tax consequences. When, in the previous chapter, the special rules relating to the early years and the closing years of a partnership were explained it was mentioned that every change in the partners could have the effect of bringing these rules into operation. This chapter is devoted to a consideration of this important practical aspect of partnership taxation; the chapter is concerned more with the tax planning aspects of partnership changes than with the fine details of the tax mathematics involved.

The Basic Rule and the Alternative Approach

The tax statutes set out a simple basic rule dealing with a change in the partners of a firm: whenever there is a change in the partners (whether it be a new partner joining or an old partner retiring or dying) the firm is to be regarded as having closed on the date of the change and then immediately re-opened as a new business. This will bring into effect all of the special rules relating to the closing years and the early years which were fully discussed in the previous chapter.

But, because a closure and an immediate re-opening may produce income tax consequences to the overall disadvantage of the firm, the tax statutes permit an alternative approach: the firm may, if it wishes, make an application (usually known as a notice of election) to its Inspector of Taxes that the income tax assessments should continue to be calculated on the preceding-year basis just as if there had been no change in the partners. The notice of election must be signed by all the persons who were partners both before and after the change or (in the case of a deceased partner) by his executors or administrators.

For the sake of technical completeness, it should be mentioned that the alternative approach is only permissible if there is at least one person who is common to the partnership both before and after the change. In the extremely rare instance where all of the partners retire and are replaced by a completely new set of partners the basic rule mentioned above will apply and there is no opportunity for the firm to adopt the alternative approach.

This discussion of the basic rule and the alternative approach applies equally where a one-man business takes in a partner or partners thereby becoming a partnership and to the converse situation where all of the partners of a firm except one retire so that the firm becomes a one-man business.

If the partnership wishes to adopt the alternative approach it must submit its notice of election within a time limit which is strictly adhered to in practice by the Inland Revenue: the notice of election must be sent to the Inspector of Taxes within two years of the date of the change in the partners.

Which Method Should You Adopt?

Two years is not a very long time to come to an informed decision whether or not a notice of election should be submitted. The decision will rest upon a comparison of the amount of partnership profits just before the change with the amounts afterwards.

If a notice of election is not submitted, so that the partnership is treated as having closed and re-opened, then (using the unofficial terminology adopted in the previous chapter) there will be a pass-over period in the old partnership and a multiplication of profits in the new partnership. Because the subject was extensively covered with examples in the previous chapter, it is unnecessary to give more figures here but it will be apparent that if the tax benefit of the pass-over period in the old partnership exceeds the tax disadvantage of the multiplication of profits in the new partnership then a notice of election will not be submitted because there will be an overall advantage in bringing into play the closing years rules followed by the early years rules.

In very broad and general terms, it will be advantageous not to submit a notice of election and to let the closing years rules and opening years rules apply where profits have been falling away around about the time of the partnership change; and, conversely, it will generally be an advantage to submit a notice of election where profits are on a rising graph.

In practice, of course, a decision whether or not to submit a notice of election will be made after the firm's tax accountants have calculated the income tax assessments for all of the relevant years first by applying one method and then the other. The decision will normally be to adopt whichever of the two methods gives the lower total income tax assessments; the general description in the previous paragraphs is designed to assist the reader to understand the overall practical effect of the choice of methods. In some instances, the two different methods will produce income tax assessments which, in total, do not vary very much from each other. When this happens it is advisable not to make the decision simply on the basis of the respective total income tax assessments. The tax accountant should calculate the actual amount of income tax payable by the partnership for each of the relevant years under each of the two methods and base the decision on a comparison of the two totals of income tax payable. This is important because such things as changes in the rates of tax between one year and another can have a marked effect on the total taxes payable.

Planning a Change in the Partners

Instances arise in practice where a properly timed change in the partners of a firm can produce tax benefits. This will be the case when the pattern of profits is such that a closure and an immediate re-commencement will reduce the total income tax assessments. The following example demonstrates the point.

Example 5.1.
Suppose that a two-partner firm has been in business since 1950 preparing annual accounts to 31 March, and that the profits in recent years have been as listed below. (The figures below are the amounts of profit as adjusted for income tax purposes but before deducting tax depreciation allowances. As was explained in the previous chapter, under the heading "Tax depreciation allowances", the income tax assessments shown in this example will in practice be reduced by capital allowances; the capital allowances are not shown in the example as this would obscure the prime lesson of the example for many readers. For similar reasons, no account is taken in the example of the "stock relief" which would probably be given in practice – this relief is explained in chapter 8.)

Year ending 31 March 1972	£15,000
Year ending 31 March 1973	17,000
Year ending 31 March 1974	16,500
Year ending 31 March 1975	19,000
Year ending 31 March 1976	8,000
Year ending 31 March 1977	300
Year ending 31 March 1978	26,000
Total profits for the seven years	£101,800

The income tax assessments on these profits will be arrived at using the preceding-year basis fully explained in the previous chapter:-

1972/73	£15,000
1973/74	17,000
1974/75	16,500
1975/76	19,000
1976/77	8,000
1977/78	300
1978/79	26,000
Total income tax assessments	£101,800

But suppose now that a third partner joined the firm on

1 April 1976. If no notice of election was submitted to the Inspector of Taxes the income tax assessments would be calculated as if the partnership had closed on 1 April 1976 and immediately re-opened on the same day. The income tax assessments for the seven years listed above would be as follows:-

Old partnership –

1972/73	preceding-year basis	£15,000
1973/74	actual profits earned in the income tax year	16,500 approx
1974/75	actual profits earned in the income tax year	19,000 approx
	(note that for 1973/74 and 1974/75 the Inland Revenue would use the actual profits basis as this gives higher assessments than the preceding-year basis)	
1975/76	actual profits	8,000 approx

New partnership –

1975/76	actual profits	Nil approx
1976/77	profits of first 12 months	300
1977/78	preceding-year basis	300
1978/79	preceding-year basis	26,000
Total income tax assessments for the seven years		£85,100

The partners have the legal right to submit a notice of election, in which case the change in the partners would be effectively ignored and the assessments for the seven years would all be on the preceding-year basis totalling £101,800 as shown above. Of course, in this particular instance the notice of election would not be submitted.

Bringing in the third partner on 1 April 1976 has had the effect of reducing the total income tax assessments by £16,700. In simple terms, this is because the closure and re-opening of the partnership has created the tax disadvantage of multiplication of profits during a period of low profits and the tax advantage of a pass-over period based on much higher profits. The example demonstrates the tax saving that can sometimes be made by arranging a change of partners at about the time that profits begin to tail off.

The Form of a Notice of Election

There is no official form available for giving a notice of election and in practice Inspectors of Taxes are not usually overconcerned about the precise wording used so long as the general intention is quite clear. However, because the author is aware that a number of partnerships and their advisers are sometimes uncertain how to prepare a notice of election, a suggested form is given below:-

H.M. Inspector of Taxes, 1 June 1979
Blankshire District.

Dear Sir,

In connection with the change which took place on 30 June 1977 when Mr AB retired from the partnership business carried on in the name of CD & Partners, we hereby elect under the provisions of Section 154 (2) Income and Corporation Taxes Act 1970 that Section 154(1) of that Act shall not apply to the change.

Yours faithfully,
(to be signed by all the persons who were partners immediately before and immediately after the change.)

A word of advice based on practical experience. If possible, it should be arranged that as soon as a change in partners takes place a notice of election in the above or similar form is signed by all the parties. This should not be sent to the Inspector of Taxes but it should be held in safe keeping by the partnership secretary or the partnership's tax accountants. When, at some later time, the two different methods of calculating the firm's income tax assessments are compared the notice of election can either be submitted to the Inspector of Taxes or destroyed as the case may be. This avoids the eleventh-hour panic of obtaining signatures from partners just before the time limit expires.

What if a Partner Refuses to Sign?

In the discussion so far in this chapter it has been assumed that the decision whether to submit a notice of election or not will be made by comparing the income tax payable by the firm under each of the two methods. But this is really an oversimplification because it does not take account of the fact that one method may be better for one partner but worse for another. It is not unusual to find a situation where a partner has retired from a firm and all the remaining partners want to submit a notice of election to obtain a substantial tax advantage but the retiring partner does not wish to sign one because it puts him at a tax disadvantage. It is suggested that in such circumstances the best course to follow is for the notice of election to be signed by all, and for the partners to whom the election is an advantage to make some financial compensation to the partner who suffers the disadvantage.

To take the point a stage further, it is recommended that the partnership agreement includes a provision requiring the retiring partner (or the executors or administrators of a deceased partner) to sign a notice of election if asked to do so, so long as he is compensated for any additional tax burden falling upon him as a result of signing the election.

Changes in Salaried Partners

Towards the end of chapter 3 there was a brief discussion about salaried partners. The subject is a difficult one for a book of a general nature since in some firms salaried partners are no more than superior employees and are not treated as partners for tax purposes whereas in other firms salaried partners are regarded for tax in the same way as what are often called full partners.

The discussion in this chapter of the effect of a change in partners has been concerned only with changes in those persons who are treated as full partners for tax purposes. If salaried partners in a particular firm are regarded as no more than superior employees for tax then the elevation of a member of the staff to the status of salaried partner will not bring into play the rules discussed in this chapter. But the elevation of such a salaried partner to the rank of full partner will bring the rules into play.

Tax Depreciation Allowances: "Stock Relief"

For completeness, it is mentioned that the effect of changes in the partners on the calculation of tax depreciation allowances is dealt with towards the end of the next chapter. And chapter 8 includes a comment on the choices available in regard to "stock relief" when there is a partnership change.

CHAPTER SIX

TAX ALLOWANCES FOR CAPITAL EXPENDITURE PART I – BUSINESS EQUIPMENT, MACHINERY AND PLANT

Introducing Capital Allowances

In the examples in chapter 4 and chapter 5 the income tax assessments were shown in a number of hypothetical situations. The point was made that in practice allowances would be deducted from those assessments to cover depreciation of capital expenditure. These tax depreciation allowances are known as capital allowances.

The majority of readers will be familiar with the accountancy treatment of capital expenditure (for example, the cost of buying a book-keeping machine or constructing a building) in preparing business accounts: the expenditure is not charged against profits as an ordinary expense in the business profit and loss account at the time it is incurred but it is depreciated over a number of years. In principle, the taxation treatment of business capital expenditure follows closely the accountancy treatment. The expenditure is not allowed against profits as an expense in the ordinary way (because it is capital – see chapter 3) but capital allowances are given over a period of years based on the amount of the expenditure. In some instances, as we shall see in this chapter, the rate of capital allowance write-off is 100% in the first year so that, in practical terms, the capital allowance produces the same result as if the expenditure had been written off as an ordinary business running expense.

The tax statutes set out a number of headings of expenditure on which capital allowances will be granted including such curious items as the cost of buying industrial know-how and expenditure on dredging inland waterways. The practical importance of the various headings set out in the statutes is that capital expenditure does not automatically qualify for capital allowances simply because it is capital expenditure. In broad terms, unless the expenditure comes under one of the prescribed headings it will qualify for no capital allowances at all.

Out of the many statutory categories of capital expenditure on which capital allowances are granted the most important in practice are, first, machinery and plant and second, certain buildings. This chapter and the next are devoted principally to an examination of the current system of capital allowances relating to these two important types of expenditure. The two different headings provide a marked contrast which will become fully apparent as the chapters proceed but is worth noting in this introduction. The scheme of allowances on machinery and plant is extremely generous: the rates of allowances are generally very high and the phrase "machinery and plant" is given a very wide meaning which is beneficial to the majority of partnerships. The allowances on buildings are miserly in comparison: the rate of allowance is (understandably perhaps) lower than on machinery and plant and (much more important) the definition of qualifying buildings is remarkably restricted. It is because the allowances on "machinery and plant" are so generous and so widely applied that the subject of capital allowances is nowadays of great practical importance in effective partnership tax planning.

There are a number of twists and turns in the subject and to make it intelligible to the reader this chapter will at several points touch only lightly on certain aspects and will return to them later in greater depth when an overall appreciation of capital allowances has been obtained.

What Sort of Partnership are we Discussing?

Partnerships exist, of course, for all types of business The reader may be a partner or a sole practitioner carrying on some professional activity, for example, a surveyor, a patent agent, a chartered accountant and so on. Or he may be a partner or sole trader carrying on a wholesaling, retailing or manufacturing activity, for example, he may be a wool broker, a coal factor, a proprietor of retail newsagent and confectionery shops or a chain of bakeries, or he may be a plastics manufacturer – the list is endless of course.

Because partnerships, sole practitioners and sole traders carrying on all of these varying activities will have different items of machinery and plant and different types of buildings, their practical interest in the subject of capital allowances will vary from one to another. This chapter and the next will attempt to cater for all possible partnership business activities and readers will, hopefully, be able to adapt the examples and illustrative discussions to the circumstances of their own particular firms.

What Constitutes "Machinery and Plant"?

From here on, this chapter will be concerned with the statutory heading "machinery and plant", leaving buildings to be covered in the next chapter. The question, what is "machinery and plant", has wide practical implications for partnerships. It has already been said that the capital allowances on machinery and plant are generous (just how generous will soon be explained in full) so that if a partnership has incurred an expense which has not been allowed against profits because it is capital then the firm must hope that it falls under the heading "machinery and plant".

Probably the most important authority on the interpretation of the phrase "machinery and plant" is an old case, Yarmouth v France, which, strangely enough, concerned not income tax but the liability of an employer to his employees in the event of accident. Fortunately for partnerships in modern times, this 1887 decision gave a wide interpretation to the phrase. It was said in the judgement that it included:

> " . . . . whatever apparatus is used by a businessman for carrying on his business – not his stock in trade which he buys or makes for sale; but all goods and chattels, fixed or moveable, live or dead, which he keeps for permanent employment in his business."

The generous machinery and plant allowances are therefore given not only on machinery in the accepted sense of the word but also on such items as:

- office calculators, computers, dictating machines, typewriters, accounting machines and other office equipment;
- books
- desks, chairs, carpets, curtains and other office furniture and fittings;
- cash registers, counters, shelves and other shop equipment and fittings (but not fixed shop-fronts);
- electrical installations (though not electrical wiring), central heating and air conditioning plant, hot water pipes (but not cold water pipes) and sanitary fittings;
- ships and aircraft;
- passenger cars and other motor vehicles;
- and so on.

Of the items in the above list, special mention must be made of expenditure on passenger cars. Because some special tax rules exist for such expenditure, passenger cars will be dealt with separately later in this chapter. In the rest of this chapter, the single word "equipment" will be used to cover all items of machinery and plant in the very wide income tax sense, except passenger cars.

What Allowances are Available?

All expenditure on business equipment made at the present time qualifies for a 100% allowance in the first year — officially and appropriately called a first-year allowance. The practical effect is that the full cost of equipment is written off as a deduction from taxable business profits at the outset. This substantial tax relief is given whether the equipment is new or second hand. It is also given whether it is purchased outright or on hire purchase. (The effect of buying on hire purchase is explained more fully later on in this chapter.)

"Free Depreciation"

The current system enabling a business to claim a first-year allowance of 100% is often referred to as a "free depreciation" system. This is a misnomer because this expression is normally taken to mean a system under which a business is free to take its tax depreciation in whichever year suits it best. Unfortunately, this is not so! Admittedly, the tax legislation does contain provisions for disclaiming first-year allowances, in whole or in part. Thus firms are entitled to claim only such part of the first-year allowances as they consider advantageous at the time. However, if only part of a first-year allowance is claimed, the balance of the allowance cannot be claimed in any selected subsequent year simply at the will of the firm.

For example, a partnership may buy equipment for £10,000 but may not wish to claim the whole £10,000 as an immediate first-year allowance. The partnership may decide that in its particular circumstances an allowance of (say) £3,000 is all it needs in the first year. The balance of £7,000 would be disclaimed but regrettably it cannot be claimed as a "first-year" allowance in a subsequent year. The firm is entitled only to an annual depreciation allowance, known as a writing down allowance, in subsequent years calculated at the rate of 25% on the balance of expenditure. For the second year the firm may claim an allowance of only £1,750 (that is, 25% of £7,000) and so on in subsequent years on the reducing balance.

To underline the point, these rules for disclaiming first-year allowances on equipment generally can be contrasted with the special rules existing for ships. If expenditure is incurred on a new ship the first-year allowance may be postponed either wholly or partly. The amount of the first-year allowance which has been postponed may be used in any subsequent year. This is free depreciation in the accepted sense.

Readers may wonder why a partnership should ever want to reject the generous first-year allowance wholly or in part. This is probably more readily grasped after a more comprehensive discussion of capital allowances has been completed. Later in this chapter, the subject of disclaiming allowances will be returned to under the heading "When not to claim capital allowances".

Capital Allowances are Given for Income Tax Years

In chapter 4, dealing with the question how accounting years are changed into income tax years, it was necessary to explain some features of the capital allowances system in advance of this present chapter. Readers will find it useful if they now refresh themselves on the two aspects discussed in that chapter under the heading "Tax depreciation allowances": first, that capital allowances are given in substitution for the depreciation written off in the partnership profit and loss account; second, the technical point that capital allowances are given as a deduction from the assessment for an income tax year rather than as a deduction from the profit for an accounting year.

Some expansion of this second point is now called for. If a partnership is calculating its capital allowances for, say, the income tax year 1978/79 surely it does not have to do this by looking at its additions to its equipment in the year ended 5 April 1979? (This would of course be a very clumsy approach unless, exceptionally, it prepared its business accounts to 5 April 1979). No, it does not have to look at its expenditure in the income tax year.

Suppose that the partnership prepares its accounts each year to 30 June. Then, in calculating the capital allowances for 1978/79 the partnership will look at the changes in its business equipment in the year ending 30 June 1977. This is perfectly logical since, as the reader will recall from chapter 4, the income tax assessment for 1978/79 will be the amount of profits in the accounting year ending 30 June 1977. The rule is that in calculating capital allowances for any particular income tax year a partnership will look at the changes in its equipment not in the income tax year itself but in what might reasonably be termed the related accounts year, that is, the accounting year the profits of which are taken to calculate the tax liability for the particular income tax year. This is perhaps a rather complex way of expressing what many will regard as a simple and obvious fact. It is however important that the concept of "related accounts year" be fully understood at this stage since frequent reference will be necessary to this feature of the capital allowances system in this chapter and the next. (Incidentally, the tax statutes do not actually use the phrase "related accounts year". The form of words used there is "basis period" but as this is not fully expressive it is not adopted in this book.)

Those readers who recall their struggle through the maze of special rules in chapter 4 covering the early years and closing years of a partnership business will suspect that in the field of capital allowances there are some complementary rules for ascertaining the related accounts year. Their suspicion is well-founded but space is not devoted to these rules here since they are matters of technical detail with little application in the field of partnership tax planning.

How to Qualify for the First-year Allowance

Suppose that a partnership prepares its accounts each year to 30 June and that around about April 1977 it becomes clear that it is going to have a highly profitable year ending 30 June 1977. The partners know therefore that their tax bill for the income tax year 1978/79 is going to be high. In April 1977 they turn their minds to the question whether they can reduce the 1978/79 tax bill by buying business equipment and claiming the first-year allowance. But what precisely does the partnership have to do to qualify? Is it enough if the equipment is ordered and nothing else? Or does the partnership have to take delivery of the equipment? Or pay for it? And by what date must all this be done?

These are important practical questions and they are answered in the tax statutes. In broad terms, the rule is that a partnership will qualify for the first-year allowance for any particular income tax year if, at some time during the related accounts year, it became legally liable to pay for an item of equipment and if, as a result of this, the equipment belonged to the partnership at some time during the income tax year. The rule expressed in this form, a much simplified version of the statutory wording, is nevertheless difficult to digest and what it really boils down to in the majority of cases is that a first-year allowance will be granted for an income tax year if there was a liability to pay for the equipment at some time during the related accounts year.

Therefore, the partnership that knows in April 1977 that it is going to have a profitable year ending 30 June 1977 and wishes to reduce its 1978/79 tax bill by first-year allowances can usually do so if, looking at the problem from a practical point of view, it receives an invoice for equipment not later than 30 June 1977 making itself legally liable to pay for the equipment by that date. If the partnership then delays paying its equipment supplier it will still be entitled to the first-year allowance for 1978/79.

The practical lesson of this example can be seen if one compares the result already described with what would have happened had the equipment been invoiced in July 1977 rather than in June. The amount of the capital allowance would have been the same but it would have been granted one year later against the 1979/80 tax assessment.

Contrary to widely held views, 5 April is not a significant date for partnerships in regard to the acquisition of capital assets; what matters is the closing date of the accounts year. Only in some exceptional cases, one of which is where the accounts are prepared each year to 5 April, is that date of significance for equipment acquisitions.

Hire Purchase

When equipment is acquired by way of hire purchase it does not fit neatly into the earlier discussion about the significance of the date on which a partnership becomes legally liable to pay for equipment.

It has already been mentioned that the first-year allowance is given on hire purchase transactions; the special rules laid down for hire purchase acquisitions seem to show that the Inland Revenue, having started on the creation of a generous system of capital allowances, just did not know where to stop with their bounty.

The practical effect of the rule covering hire purchase acquisitions is that the 100% first-year allowance is calculated on the full cash price of the equipment and this is *all* treated as having been spent by the partnership at the time the hire purchase arrangements are entered into, provided (as will usually be the case) that the equipment is at that time put into use for the purposes of the partnership's business.

As an example, consider a partnership that prepares its accounts each year to 31 December. The profits for the year ended 31 December 1979 will be assessed to income tax for the income tax year 1980/81. Suppose that at some time during the year ending 31 December 1979 an item of equipment with a cash price of £3,000 is acquired under hire purchase. A full £3,000 first-year allowance is available to the partnership for the income tax year 1980/81 regardless of whether the payments under the hire purchase agreement are payable over a long or short period. It can be seen that the saving of income tax resulting from the 100% allowance could in many instances exceed the actual cash instalments payable in the early years of the hire purchase agreement. This is particularly so if an item of equipment is acquired by hire purchase towards the end of an accounting year.

Regional Development Grants

There will be some instances where a partnership will receive what is known as a regional development grant towards the cost of business equipment under the Industry Act 1972. In such cases the 100% first-year allowance will nevertheless be given on the full gross cost of the equipment.

Motor Vehicles

Practising accountants who have been involved in lengthy and tedious correspondence with the Inland Revenue to justify a business claim for the use of motor cars have sometimes been heard to suggest that Inspectors of Taxes are more troublesome than traffic wardens: they are obsessed with hounding the business motorist. Whether or not this is believed, it is true that the tax statutes contain specific restrictions which deny the generous 100% first-year allowance to passenger cars. This discrimination against passenger cars operates by means of two separate restrictions which will shortly be explained. There is no discrimination though against commercial vehicles such as vans and lorries – they qualify for the full 100% first-year allowance.

Expressed more precisely, the rule is that all mechanically propelled road vehicles are subject to the two restrictions now to be discussed unless they are either:

- primarily suited for the carriage of goods, or
- not suitable to be used as private vehicles, or
- provided for hire to, or carriage of, the public.

The first restriction is to exclude the 100% first-year allowance altogether. Instead only a 25% allowance (known as a writing down allowance) is given each year. Second, there is a ceiling on the annual writing down allowance: it must not exceed £1,250 for any one year. (For cars purchased before 7 April 1976 the ceiling was, and still is, £1,000 for any one year.)

...... Inspectors of Taxes ...... are obsessed with hounding the business motorist ......

Example 6.1.

Assume that a partnership buys a car for £3,000 in its accounts year ending 30 September 1978, to be precise on 1 June 1978. It will commence to receive capital allowances on this car for the income tax year 1979/80 because the car was acquired in the related accounts year to 1979/80.

Cost of car — year ending 30 September 1978		£3,000
1979/80:	writing down allowance 25%	750
		2,250
1980/81:	writing down allowance 25%	562
		1,688
1981/82:	writing down allowance 25%	422
		1,266

and so on.

Example 6.2.
But if the car in example 6.1 cost £6,600:

Cost of car – year ending 30 September 1978		£6,600
1979/80:	writing down allowance 25% £1,650 restricted to	1,250
		5,350
1980/81:	writing down allowance 25% £1,338 restricted to	1,250
		4,100
1981/82:	writing down allowance 25%	1,025
		3,075

and so on.

Cars – The Practical Effect

The second of the restrictions referred to above is deliberately aimed at what are sometimes called quality cars; the restriction will clearly only operate where a car has cost more than £5,000. Both of the restrictions have the same broad practical effect: they do not deprive the partnership of capital allowances on cars in the long run but they slow down the timing of the income tax relief compared with expenditure on other capital assets.

Many partnership cars are used also to some extent for private purposes by the partners. It is well known that in these cases the tax relief for capital allowances will be proportionately restricted, quite apart from the two restrictions illustrated in the above examples. If, for instance, the car in example 6.2 is used occasionally by a partner for holiday travel, weekend trips and other private purposes to the extent of 10% of its total use then the tax relief based on the writing down allowances will be cut down by 10% so that for the three income tax years shown in the example the partnership will receive income tax relief on £1,125, £1,125 and £923 respectively.

This discussion of the practical effect of the capital allowances on cars is incomplete without a reference to what happens when cars are disposed of. It is not possible to do this until the next concept — the pool of expenditure — is explained.

Pool of Expenditure
All money spent on the acquisition of equipment and (subject to an exception to be mentioned later) cars is lumped together for tax purposes in one pool except to the extent that it is immediately written off by a 100% first-year allowance. Then for each income tax year the partnership is entitled to an annual writing-down allowance at the rate of 25% of the total figure standing in the pool. Individual items of equipment are not separately identified and the writing-down allowance is calculated on one composite total each year. All this will become clearer when the example below is read.

The following are the types of expenditure that in practice one finds in this pool.

1. Expenditure on cars (subject to the exception to be mentioned later).

2. Expenditure on equipment bought between October 1970 and March 1972. At that time equipment was not entitled to a 100% first-year allowance — it was 60% or 80%. Therefore, even if the partnership claimed the maximum first-year allowance there will still have been a balance of expenditure which went into the pool.

3. Expenditure on equipment bought before October 1970. That also did not qualify for a 100% first-year allowance. Up to and including the tax year 1976/77 these items had to be treated separately for capital allowance purposes and in accordance with special rules; in the tax year 1977/78 the written-down value of these items joined the general pool.

4. Expenditure on equipment bought after March 1972 where the partnership has decided not to claim the 100% first-year allowance, or not to claim it in full.

(Later on in this chapter, under the heading "When not to Claim Capital Allowances", the circumstances in which this might happen will be considered.)

Example 6.3

A partnership has been in existence for many years and makes its accounts up to 31 December. On 31 December 1973 the partnership's written-down pool of expenditure (deriving from various items bought between October 1970 and December 1973) was £2,600. On 31 December 1975 it still had various pieces of equipment which it had bought before October 1970; the written-down value of these for tax purposes on 31 December 1975 was £550.

From 1 January 1974 to 31 December 1977 the partnership buys equipment and vehicles as follows (and no other items):-

April 1974	Generator	£15,000
March 1975	Car	£3,500
December 1977	Typewriters	£2,000

The partnership, because of its own particular circumstances at the time, decided to claim no part of the 100% first-year allowance on the generator.

The capital allowances for each tax year will derive from the position in the related accounts year, as we have said. The capital allowance calculations for the tax years 1975/76, 1976/77, 1977/78 and 1978/79 are as follows:

		Pool
1975/76 (Year ending 31.12.74)		
pool brought forward		2,600
generator	£15,000	
first-year allowance 100% disclaimed		
writing-down allowance 25% of pool	———	650
		1,950
	15,000 ⟶	15,000
carried forward		16,950

brought forward		16,950
1976/77 (Year ending 31.12.75)		
car (does not qualify for the first-year allowance)		3,500
		20,450
writing-down allowance 25% of pool		5,113
		15,337
1977/78 (Year ending 31.12.76)		
written-down balance of pre-October 1970 expenditure joins pool		550
		15,887
writing-down allowance 25% of pool		3,972
		11,915
1978/79 (Year ending 31.12.77)		
typewriters	£2,000	
first-year allowance 100%	2,000	
writing-down allowance 25% of pool		2,979
		8,936

and so on.

The total capital allowances (that is both first-year allowances and writing-down allowances) on equipment and vehicles for each of the tax years in question are as follows:

1975/76	£650
1976/77	£5,113
1977/78	£3,972
1978/79	£4,979

(These figures ignore the allowances which will have been

obtained in 1975/76 and 1976/77 on the pre-October 1970 items under the special system which then applied to them).

Note that the cost of the car joins the pool in 1976/77 and its cost is reflected in the writing-down allowance for that year. But the cost of the generator joins the pool only at the end of 1975/76 and was not reflected in the writing-down allowance for 1975/76. The rule is that where a partnership *voluntarily* forgoes a first-year allowance it gets no writing-down allowance in respect of the asset until the following year.

What About Sales?

When an item is sold, the sale proceeds are simply deducted from the pool of expenditure brought forward from the previous year. Writing down allowances from that point onwards are then calculated on the reduced figure in the pool.

Example 6.4.

Continue the calculations from example 6.3 for one more year and assume that in the accounts year ending 31 December 1978 the partnership sold for £800 the typewriters that it had purchased in December 1977. Assume also (for simplicity) that there are no other additions or sales of capital assets in 1978.

The sale of the typewriters will affect the capital allowances for 1979/80 because it took place during the accounts year related to 1979/80.

	Pool
brought forward from example 6.3	£8,936
1979/80 (Year ending 31.12.78)	
proceeds of sale of typewriters	800
	8,136
writing down allowance 25% of pool	2,034
pool carried forward	£6,102

Generous Tax Treatment of Sales

Example 6.4 shows the unexpectedly charitable approach of the Inland Revenue. The practical effect of the rules regarding sales of equipment can be seen if one notes that for the year 1978/79 a first-year allowance of £2,000 has been obtained on the typewriters (example 6.3) and this is not immediately clawed back when they are sold in the following year. Of course, in the long run there will be a clawback because starting with 1979/80 the writing down allowances are reduced as a result of the sale of the typewriters. But overall there is a considerable timing advantage to the partnership.

Disposal of a Quality Car

Having dealt with sales of equipment generally, it is convenient now to return to the earlier discussion about the restricted allowances on passenger cars. It has already been explained that writing down allowances on cars must not exceed £1,250 for any one year and this was demonstrated in example 6.2.

There is a technical rule that lays down that cars costing more than £5,000 each (£4,000 each for cars purchased before 7 April 1976) are not to form part of the general pool but each such car forms its own special separate pool. This may appear baffling but the practical effect is that when a quality car is sold the sale proceeds are compared with the figure standing in the tax calculations for the car and an immediate tax adjustment is made for the balance one way or the other.

Take the car in example 6.2 which, at the end of year 3, stood at £3,075. This amount will not be incorporated in the pool but will show up as a separate figure in the individual tax calculations applicable to the particular car. Suppose that in year 4 the car is sold for £2,500. The deficit of £575 will be allowed as a capital allowance for year 4. If, on the other hand, the sale proceeds in year 4 are £3,500 then, predictably enough, the income tax assessment on the firm will be increased by £425.

In many ways, the practical effect of all this is to negate the impact of the restricted allowances on quality cars. While the car is being used by the partnership the allowances are restricted to £1,250 a year; the effect of this is to increase the figure at which the car stands in the partnership's tax calculations so that the allowances "lost" each year because of the restriction will be "picked up" when the car is disposed of. Over the total period of ownership of the car, the total capital allowances obtained will equal the net cost (that is, the purchase price less the sale proceeds) of the car. The restrictions simply slow down the timing of the tax relief.

When not to Claim Capital Allowances

Earlier in this chapter, under the heading "Free depreciation", it was explained that a partnership need not necessarily take all or any of its first-year allowance and if it chooses not to do so then it will obtain writing down allowances in the future on the expenditure. This can be seen in operation in example 6.3 : by disclaiming the first-year allowance of £15,000 on the generator for the year 1975/76, the writing down allowances for the years commencing 1976/77 are considerably higher than they would otherwise have been.

It may seem strange to suggest that partnerships should consider spurning the benevolence offered by the Inland Revenue but there are a number of instances where accepting the first-year allowance in full could be an overall disadvantage. For instance, take the partnership referred to in example 6.3. It may be that this is a richly profitable partnership and the partners will therefore normally pay tax as a high rate. Suppose, though, that for the income tax year 1975/76 the income tax assessment is unusually low, for some exceptional reason, so that the tax rate on the partners comes down from, say, normally around 75% to around 40%. If the partnership claims the first-year allowance for 1975/76 on the generator it will obtain tax relief on £15,000 at 40%. If it disclaims the allowance it will obtain higher writing down allowances in subsequent years which will be relieved at 75%. Of course, the differing timing of the allowances has to be borne in mind but this simple illustration shows the principle to be considered.

Put very simply, the lesson is that where in a particular year a partnership has a heavy investment in equipment relative to the profit for that year it is sensible to do the arithmetic in some detail so that the tax saved by claiming the first-year allowance can be measured and compared with the projected future tax saved if the first-year allowance were rejected wholly or in part. It is especially important to do this because of a procedural aspect of rejecting the first-year allowance. In the discussion in this chapter so far, reference has sometimes been made (as a term of convenience) to "disclaiming" the allowance. But, strictly speaking, a partnership does not disclaim its first-year allowance, in the sense of submitting a formal disclaimer notice to the Inland Revenue indicating that the allowance is not wanted. The procedure is that the partnership that does not wish to take the full first-year allowance deliberately fails to claim the full amount in submitting its capital allowance workings.

It is very easy for the tax accountant who has the task of preparing the capital allowance workings to automatically claim the first-year allowance almost as a matter of habit: and the Inland Revenue take the view that a claim, once made, legally cannot be withdrawn. A partnership should if possible look at the figures carefully before putting in for a first-year allowance.

In an ideally planned situation, refusing first-year allowances would not arise because partnerships would have adopted the advice given earlier in this chapter under the heading "How to qualify for the first-year allowance" and would have timed their purchases of equipment to coincide with high tax years. But the ideal is not always achieved and the right to refuse allowances is a useful insurance against major errors of timing.

With regard to the annual writing down allowance there is a similar right for the partnership to refuse the allowance or to claim only part of it.

Adjustments between the Partners

Somewhat related to the point made under the previous heading is the effect that capital allowances now have on the partners' individual pockets. The 100% first-year allowance has a distorting effect in that it usually produces an income tax assessment which differs considerably from the profit shown by the business accounts. Suppose that a partnership spends £100,000 on a computer in its accounting year ending 30 September 1977. It may write off £25,000 of the cost of the computer against its profits for accounting purposes but, for tax purposes, the income tax assessment for 1978/79 can be reduced by £100,000. If, say, at the end of 1979 one of the partners were to retire he would have had the full benefit of his share of the £100,000 capital allowance even though the computer was still part of the partnership assets at the time he retired and would continue to be so perhaps for some years. The partners as between themselves might consider that it was unfair that he should receive a tax benefit based on the full £100,000.

This sort of situation could, in theory, be remedied by claiming a first-year allowance of only part of the £100,000 under the rules already explained but this may not be sensible from a tax point of view. Another solution may lie in the application of the technical rules discussed later in this chapter under the heading "Capital allowances and partnership changes". But often the best and simplest answer, if the partners consider that the position is unfairly weighted in favour of the retiring partner, is for some arrangement to be made between the partners themselves to make an adjustment for the distorted income tax relief. This is more an accounting point rather than a technical income tax point but it is often overlooked as between individual partners.

"Renewals Basis"

All of the explanations so far in this chapter on income tax allowances for capital expenditure have concentrated on the scheme of capital allowances. There is however an alternative approach known as the "renewals basis". Under this basis, a partnership may, at its option, select a particular category of equipment and exclude that category completely from its capital allowance workings. And then, as and when the partnership renews items of equipment within the particular category, it can treat the cost of renewal as an ordinary business expense which is allowable in the usual way in calculating the firm's taxable profit.

The renewals basis has the considerable merit of completely avoiding the preparation of detailed calculations of capital allowances and because of this some partnerships find the basis attractive. This alternative method is often found in use in regard to typewriters and similar items of office equipment.

Whatever the merits of the renewals basis may be, it has a substantial disadvantage which is not always recognised. It is based on the allowance of a tax deduction when an item of equipment is replaced so that by definition no tax allowance can be claimed under this method when the original item of equipment is acquired for the first time.

Suppose, for example, that the partnership in example 6.3 used the renewals basis for office typewriters and that the expenditure of £2,000 in December 1977 was for five electric typewriters to be used in a new branch office opened by the firm. The renewals basis would grant no deduction for the expenditure of £2,000 because it clearly was not a renewal. And remember that if the renewals basis is used it must extend to all items of equipment under a particular category so that it would not be possible for the partnership to claim capital allowances on the five typewriters because that would be mixing the two bases.

From our practical experience of examining the tax strategy of a number of partnerships, we are able to say that the use of the renewals basis is probably reasonably widespread and that its disadvantages are, in some instances, considerable in terms of additional income tax. It is possible to change from the renewals basis to a capital allowances basis and any partnerships operating the renewals basis should take advice on whether it would be to their advantage to switch the methods in future.

Tax Allowances on Leasing Equipment and Cars

Purists will object that the subject of leasing ought not to be included in this chapter. They will argue that leasing rentals are not capital expenditure. While this is undeniably correct, it is often the case that a partnership business considers the choice between buying an asset or leasing it and, in some instances, the decision becomes confused because of mistaken notions about the tax consequences. It is therefore opportune to consider at this point how lease rentals are dealt with in the context of a lease-or-buy decision.

In general, rentals for leasing business equipment and vehicles are deducted from profits as ordinary business expenses for tax purposes.

There is an apparent exception in the case of quality cars

— where the whole retail price when new was £5,000 or more. In the case of such a car on the face of it only a percentage of the hire charge is an allowable expense — the percentage depends on what the car's price when new was — with no tax relief for the balance. But there is an established loophole in the legislation, recognised by the Inland Revenue, which means that this restriction does not apply in the case of a car hired from an ordinary leasing concern. If the car were hired from, say, a leasing company owned by the partners themselves the restriction might apply.

Equipment and Vehicles — Lease or Buy?

A decision whether to lease or buy must, of course include a comparison of the total gross costs of each method. It must also take account of the cash flow aspect of the timing of the payments under the different methods. These are non-tax aspects.

Also to be taken into account are the amounts of the tax allowances and their timing. To assist readers to carry out the arithmetic in a lease-or-buy decision without the confusion over the income tax factors that is so often created by promotional literature, a simple summarised comparison table is set out below based on the explanations in this chapter. In the table, the phrase "net cost" is used to indicate the cost of purchase of an item of equipment or vehicle less its ultimate sale proceeds.

LEASE OR BUY? — THE TAX ASPECTS COMPARED		
	Leasing	Purchase, including Hire Purchase
Passenger cars costing more than £5,000	Full rentals allowed provided the car is leased from an ordinary leasing concern	Full net cost allowed in the long run
Other passenger cars	Full rentals allowed	Full net cost allowed in the long run
All other equipment and vehicles	Full rentals allowed	Full cost allowed in first year. Adjustment made when sold with the effect that the full net cost is allowed in the long run

Capital Allowances and Partnership Changes

This chapter ends with two somewhat technical matters of special concern to partnerships in particular situations. First is the effect on capital allowances of changes of partners.

In chapter 5 it was shown that where a new partner joins a partnership or an existing partner leaves there is, in general terms, a choice between treating the partnership as having closed and then re-opened or as having continued regardless of the change. What effect does either of these choices have on the partnership capital allowance workings?

If the partnership is treated as continuing then, reasonably enough, the capital allowance workings continue undisturbed. The rules covering the situation where the partnership is treated as having closed and re-opened are contained in a bewildering criss-cross of legislation. But in simple practical terms the rules effectively provide that the equipment and vehicles owned by the old partnership shall be treated for capital allowances as if they had been sold to the new partnership, normally at their market value. The new partnership is, however, only to be entitled to claim writing down allowances on the notional purchase price and not first-year allowances. The old and the new partnerships are given the right to apply to the Inland Revenue to ignore all this and to continue the capital allowance calculation from the old firm into the new firm just as if there had been no change. In practice, it is often the case that this continuing basis of calculating capital allowances is adopted automatically and without formality. This is obviously the easy thing to do but if a situation arises (as sometimes happens) where the calculations show that there is an overall tax advantage if the strict rules are applied and the equipment and vehicles are treated as sold by the old partnership to the new then this should be insisted upon in the calculations submitted to the Inland Revenue.

Assets Belonging to an Individual Partner

The second specific partnership situation is that where an item of equipment or a vehicle is used by the partnership business but is owned by an individual partner. Probably the most common instance of this is where each individual partner pays for his motor car out of his own pocket (usually so that he can have complete freedom of personal choice) and the cars are then used for business purposes without the firm paying any form of rental charge to the partners. In this type of case capital allowances can be claimed on the individually owned cars in precisely the same way as if they were owned by the firm; this is the sort of claim that is easily overlooked in some cases in practice.

Chapter 6 – Action Reminders

1. "Machinery and plant" has a wide meaning. Don't miss claiming the generous capital allowances on less obvious items, for example, office carpets and curtains.
2. Watch the correct timing of equipment purchases. The critical test usually is: was the partnership legally liable to pay for the equipment by the end of the accounting year? If the liability to pay has been incurred by the end of the year but payment is made in the following year, draw the attention of the partnership accountant to the item so that he is alerted to placing it in the correct year.
3. Hire purchase : the tax treatment here is especially favourable. Take advantage of it.
4. Beware of claiming capital allowances up to the hilt in a year when profits are relatively modest compared to the amount of equipment purchased. Ensure that the present *and future* consequences of claiming and not claiming are calculated as closely as possible and compared. And that this is done *before* the capital allowance claims are submitted.
5. Is your firm using the renewals basis on any items of equipment? If so, take advice on whether there would be a worth-while tax saving from changing to a capital allowance basis.
6. Lease-or-buy decisions: use the table in this chapter to cut through any confusion over the tax consequences.
7. Don't forget to claim capital allowances on motor cars (and, if applicable, other items) owned by individual partners but used by the firm.

CHAPTER SEVEN

TAX ALLOWANCES FOR CAPITAL EXPENDITURE PART II – BUILDINGS

A Chapter You Should Not Skip!

By comparison with the liberal scheme of capital allowances on equipment discussed in the previous chapter, the allowances on buildings will be disappointing. In particular, because of the very limited category of buildings that qualify for any capital allowances at all, many partnerships will obtain little or no relief on their expenditure on buildings. This will apply particularly to partnerships carrying on professional practices.

This chapter will, therefore, deal only briefly with the capital allowances on buildings. Because of the limited application of the subject, the description will be in general terms without the extensive examples used in previous chapters; the explanation will concentrate on those areas where action may produce tax savings. As the chapter develops it will become clear that it will be of greatest application to partnerships engaged in some manufacturing activity but those readers who are therefore tempted to shut their eyes completely to the chapter are urged to read at least the section headed "When is a building not a building?" since this is of wide application and incorporates some thoughts for reducing the partnership tax bill.

Industrial Buildings

Regrettably, the tax statutes do not refer to capital allowances on "buildings" but, in the main, to allowances only on "industrial buildings and structures". This latter phrase is defined in a very restricted way. The definition is of great importance since, apart from a minor exception or two, expenditure on constructing or buying a business building will give rise to no income tax allowances at all unless the building qualifies as a member of this favoured class, industrial buildings and structures.

To determine whether a building qualifies one must consider both the type of business carried on by the partnership and the nature of the building.

If, at this stage of the explanation, you wish to consider whether a particular building owned by your firm qualifies as an industrial building, the question may be approached in the form adopted in the highly simplified chart that follows. The chart ignores special situations and is explained in the succeeding paragraphs.

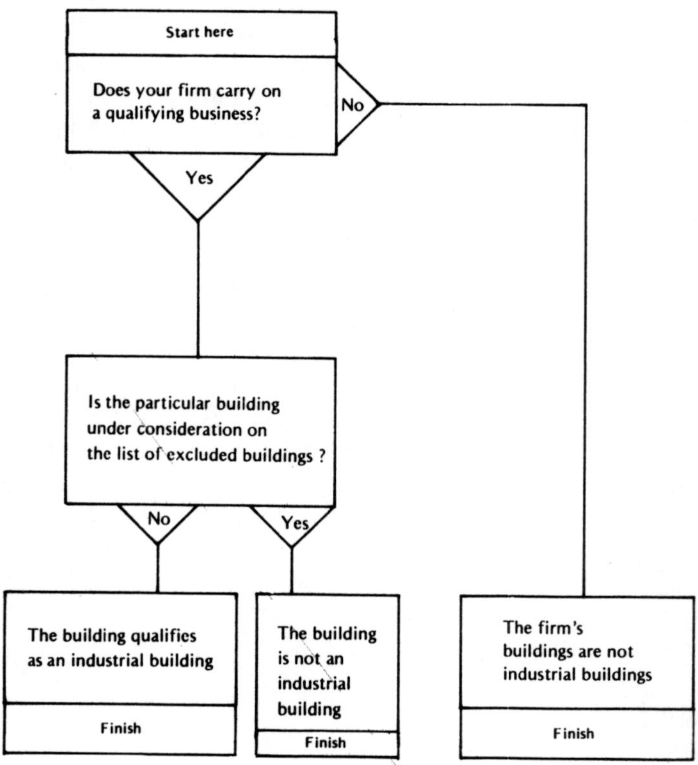

With regard to the first question in the chart, tax legislation contains a list of those businesses which qualify, principally the manufacturing or processing of goods or materials. If your business is not within the stated categories no capital allowances on buildings will be given (subject to an exception mentioned later). If your business does qualify, however, it cannot be assumed that buildings allowances will be given on all of your buildings since you now have to move to the next question in the chart: is the particular building excluded? The legislation contains a list of excluded buildings, principally offices, showrooms and retail shops. It can therefore be seen that there is a vast range of buildings for which no tax depreciation is allowed: some examples are the office premises of a manufacturing business and the buildings of a department store.

There is a particular aspect of the dividing line between qualifying and non-qualifying buildings that deserves mention because of its practical implications. As was explained above, the processing of goods or materials qualifies and it is easy to overlook the fact that there are some partnerships whose activities could probably be brought within the word "processing" so as to qualify them for allowances on some of their buildings.

Processing Activities

Consider, for example, the 1966 case of Kilmarnock Equitable Co-operative Society Limited v. Inland Revenue. In this case, the company sold pre-packed coal. The coal was carried from wagons into a hopper on a conveyor belt, dross was then removed and the coal was weighed and packed into bags. The Court decided that this constituted a process in the income tax sense of the word and that the company was entitled to industrial buildings allowances. Practical experience in this particular area of tax shows that there are a number of trading partnerships that could usefully re-examine the category into which their trading activities have been placed. But as an extension of the exclusion of retail shops already mentioned, wholly retail organisations will unfortunately not be able to benefit.

A macabre incidental comment on this topic: one business that did re-examine its category was Norwich Crematorium! In the 1967 case of Bourne v. Norwich Crematorium Limited, probably the only tax case that could be described as spine-chilling, the company argued that it fell into the category of a processor of goods or materials because it converted human corpses into ashes. The company lost its argument but principally on the grounds that a corpse was not "goods or materials". The judge also refused to be influenced by the company's rather subtle alternative contention that it was processing shrouds and coffins!

A Special Case

There is an exception to the rules. For reasons that are difficult to fathom, staff sports pavilions are awarded special beneficial treatment by the tax legislation. They are entitled to allowances as industrial buildings so long as they are occupied by a trading organisation as distinct from a professional practice, even if the trade is not a qualifying trade. Because this provision is tucked away in the small print of the legislation it is easily overlooked. A retail partnership, for example, should ensure that capital allowances are claimed on a sports pavilion if the firm is large enough to have one.

Buildings Partly Industrial

Where part of a building does not qualify (a simple example is the case of a wholesale bakery with one floor devoted to administrative offices) the total cost of the building must be split between the qualifying and non-qualifying parts and allowances will be given on the qualifying part only. But to obviate the time-consuming task of making apportionments in trivial cases the rules provide that if the non-qualifying part is 10% or less of the total then the *whole* building is treated as qualifying. In strict law the 10% comparison should be made by reference to the respective construction costs of the qualifying and non-qualifying parts of the building but in practice the comparison is often made in terms of floor area.

The 10% rule effectively permits allowances to be claimed on non-qualifying expenditure when it is mixed in with qualifying expenditure. It is a rule which can sometimes usefully be borne in mind when a partnership is in the early planning stage of building construction.

What Allowances are Available?

Expenditure on a *new* industrial building qualifies for two separate allowances: a once-only initial allowance in the first year; and a writing down allowance which is also given in the first year and then in subsequent years on an annual basis.

The rate of initial allowance applicable to expenditure after 12 November 1974 is 50%; it was lower previously. This allowance is given only to the owner of a new or unused building, not to the purchaser of a used building.

The annual writing down allowance is 4% of the cost of the building; the allowance is calculated on the cost of the building not only in the first year but in all subsequent years. (For buildings first used before 6 November 1962 the rate of writing down allowance is only 2% of cost each year.)

Buying a Used Building

It is important to note that the form of the allowances briefly described above is applicable only where a partnership constructs an industrial building or buys an unused industrial building.

Where a partnership buys a used building it will not receive allowances in the form considered above. Firstly, there will be no initial allowance – this is available only for the building in its original new state. Secondly, the writing down allowance is computed in a totally different manner. Commonsense would suggest that the writing down allowance would be calculated on the amount paid by the purchaser for the building. But this will rarely happen in practice. The subject is one of considerable technical complexity but, broadly speaking, the purchaser of a used industrial building will only be able to calculate his annual writing down allowances on the *lower* of two figures: 1, the purchase price of the building to him, and 2, the original cost of construction of the building. Clearly, this will usually produce a totally unfair tax result to the purchaser.

When is a Building Not a Building?

A comparison between the scheme of capital allowances for equipment explained in the previous chapter and the allowances given for buildings reveals a marked preference by the powers-that-be for expenditure on equipment. Whereas expenditure on equipment is generally allowed for tax immediately, expenditure on industrial buildings, after the initial allowance of 50%, is written off at a relatively slow rate of 4% per annum. Even more importantly, a great number of business buildings (including probably all the buildings used by many partnerships) fail to attract any form of capital allowance at all.

Well, when is a building not a building? The answer is: when it's really equipment. The business partner and the partnership tax accountant with tax saving in mind should take great care to classify capital expenditure into the two categories, equipment on the one hand and buildings on the other, in the most advantageous way for tax purposes, so far as this can properly be done.

For example, a partnership might build a small office block for £250,000. In the partnership's balance sheet this figure would in all probability be shown under one heading, land and buildings. But for tax it is important to analyse the total expenditure into its constituent parts. A breakdown of the £250,000 might be as follows:

Land	£100,000
Structure, excluding the items listed below	108,000
Lift	19,000
Central heating and hot water system, including hot water pipes	5,000
Electrical fittings (but not wiring)	1,000
Toilets and fittings, mirrors, etc.	2,000
Floor coverings	2,000
Moveable internal partitioning	13,000
	£250,000

Of the items listed in the breakdown, the first amount of £100,000 for land qualifies for no capital allowances. If you find this surprising the reason is stated at the opening of chapter 6 where capital allowances were introduced: the tax statutes set out the headings of expenditure on which capital allowances are granted and, unfortunately, land is not to be found amongst these statutory headings. Next in the list, the amount of £108,000 for the structure does not attract capital allowances as the building is an office block which does not qualify.

"Right, here's £99,000 for the mirrors in the toilets and £1,000 for the rest of the building."

The remaining items would all be regarded as equipment qualifying for a first-year allowance of 100%. The reader is reminded that although the description "equipment" has been used in this book as a convenient expression, the correct phrase (as explained in chapter 6) is "machinery and plant". The wide meaning of this statutory expression was discussed in chapter 6.

The tax saving involved in successfully pursuing such an argument is obvious and yet it is often overlooked in practice. It is not necessary to make the allocation suggested in the partnership balance sheet. The balance sheet can continue to show the item of £250,000 as, for example, land and buildings, if this is preferred. This will not prejudice a tax claim to treat part of the expenditure as qualifying for the 100% first-year allowance on equipment.

The last item in the list (partitioning) justifies some further comment because it is often met with in partnership businesses and it is sometimes the subject of disagreement with the Inland Revenue. The 1962 case of Jarrold v.

John Good & Sons Ltd may well be of assistance to partnerships who are faced with this problem. John Good & Sons Ltd had several departments to its business and the work of each department fluctuated from time to time. The company therefore took premises with open floor space and divided it with partitions that were screwed to the floor and the ceiling but were removable; the divided floor space had a flexible nature to suit the nature of the business. The company claimed capital allowances on the expenditure on the partitions, treating the items as equipment but the Inland Revenue refused the claims by arguing that the partitions were part of the setting in which the business was carried on and were therefore buildings for tax purposes. The company claimed that the partitions were part of the business "apparatus" and were machiney and plant and not buildings. The Court decided in favour of the company and treated the partitions as machinery and plant.

CHAPTER 7

TAX MITIGATION CHECK-LIST

Buildings used in a processing business may qualify for tax depreciation allowances. Is your business on the borderlines of "processing"? You may be able to reduce your firm's tax bill by arguing with your tax inspector that "processing" has a wider than normal meaning for tax purposes.

Your partnership balance sheet probably includes a heading of expenditure such as "Land and Buildings". Don't overlook the substantial tax relief that may be locked up here and which may perhaps be released by a re-classification of the expenditure — dig deep for items which can properly be classified as machinery or plant.

CHAPTER EIGHT

TAX RELIEF FOR INCREASED INVESTMENT IN WORK-IN-PROGRESS AND STOCK

What is This Thing Called Stock Relief?

"Stock relief" is a comparatively new animal. In an era of inflation businesses — even if they are not expanding — have to lock up not merely gross receipts but profit too in investment in new work-in-progress or trade stock. In 1975 the Chancellor of the Exchequer brought in changes in tax law which go quite a long way towards compensating for this. The basic idea behind the relief is simple. Instead of charging income tax on the full amount of partnership profits a deduction is given which is measured broadly speaking by the partnership's increased investment in work-in-progress and stock.

This chapter explains the way in which the relief works. Although it is generally known as stock relief, it applies to professional work-in-progress as well as to trade stock, though there are one or two minor differences in the treatment of the two. Because the majority of readers of this book are likely to be concerned with the tax position of professional practices, the chapter will discuss the subject in the context of work-in-progress only; readers concerned with merchanting and manufacturing businesses will easily be able to adapt the explanation to business stock. But although the discussion in this chapter is centred on professional work-in-progress the relief will be referred to throughout as stock relief to conform with its usual description.

One feature of the relief in particular is of enormous

practical significance. The relief cannot be regarded as a permanent reduction in tax liability; it is really no more than an indefinite *deferral* of tax. This is because the stock relief rules contain provisions which claw-back the relief when, at some future time, the partnership's investment in work-in-progress falls. The precise way in which this works will be explained in the examples in this chapter.

Before proceeding, it is worth making the perhaps obvious point that if a partnership does not carry work-in-progress in its balance sheet and accounts then there can be no entitlement to stock relief. Strictly speaking, accounts for tax purposes should include each year a figure for work-in-progress which is normally calculated as the costs incurred on those jobs or assignments which have not yet been billed to clients. In practice, different firms adopt a variety of procedures for arriving at the figure and the Inland Revenue will generally agree to any procedure which is fair and reasonable and is applied consistently from one year to another. But there are some professional firms who, by agreement with the Inspector of Taxes, have by-passed the whole problem and who prepare accounts without bringing in work-in-progress. As was said earlier, such firms cannot of course claim stock relief.

The Rules Explained

Because stock relief is substantially an arithmetical subject, its workings can best be understood by way of an example followed by an explanation of the rules applied in the example.

Example 8.1

An old-established firm of consulting engineers prepares its accounts to 31 December. The firm wishes to calculate its entitlement to stock relief for the year ending 31 December 1976. Stock relief given for previous years totalled £50,000.

The relevant information for the year ending 31 December 1976 is as follows:-

Work-in-progress at 1 January 1976	£65,000
Work-in-progress at 31 December 1976	105,000

Profit for year ending 31 December 1976 as adjusted for tax purposes but before deducting stock relief or tax depreciation allowances (capital allowances)	110,000
Capital allowances for 1977/78	10,000

Stock relief based on the year ending 31 December 1976 is calculated as follows:-

Increase in work-in-progress over the year (£105,000 – £65,000)	£ 40,000
Less 15% of (profit less capital allowances) (£110,000 – £10,000)	15,000
Stock relief	£ 25,000

The income tax assessment on the firm for 1977/78 will finally be:-

Profit		£110,000
Less Stock relief	£25,000	
Capital allowances	10,000	35,000
Tax payable on		£75,000

The calculation of stock relief proceeds in two steps. They are:

1. find the increase in work-in-progress by deducting the balance sheet value at the beginning of the year from the balance sheet value at the end of the year. If there is no increase, then there is no stock relief – this position will be examined in example 8.2 below;

2. deduct from the increase in the value of work-in-progress, 15% of the business profits. For this purpose, the business profits are the figures as adjusted for tax and after deducting capital allowances. Only the profits arising from carrying on the particular profession or

trade are brought into account in calculating the 15% deduction, so that if, for example, a partnership invests its surplus cash in property purely to receive the letting income the rents received would not form part of the profit in calculating the 15% deduction. The answer at the end of this second step is the stock relief.

In many partnerships, clients make payments on account while work-in-progress is building up. The figures of work-in-progress to be taken into account in the stock relief calculations are the amounts after deducting any payments on account which have been received.

The above example has deliberately dealt with the normal situation of an established business preparing its accounts for twelve months at a time. The tax statutes contain a number of technical rules dealing with the calculation of stock relief in special situations such as on the opening of a new business, the closing down of a business and the changing of an annual accounting date. These situations all create difficult problems but it is outside the scope of this practical guide to discuss them in detail.

The rules as we have explained them apply to accounting years ending after 5 April 1975. Stock relief has, broadly speaking, applied for all accounting years ending since 6 April 1973, but the rules for the first two years were a little different.

The next example continues from the facts in example 8.1 in the following year; the explanation follows the example.

Example 8.2

In 1978, the firm of consulting engineers in example 8.1 considers its entitlement to stock relief for the year ending 31 December 1977. Had there been a sufficient increase in its work-in-progress over the year 1977 the firm would have been entitled to stock relief but in fact there has been a contraction of business during the year and the relevant figures are as follows:-

Work-in-progress at 1 January 1977	£105,000
Work-in-progress at 31 December 1977	70,000

Profit for year ending 31 December 1977 as adjusted for tax purposes but before deducting stock relief or tax depreciation allowances (capital allowances)	60,000
Capital allowances 1978/79	6,000

Because work-in-progress has fallen over the year there will be a claw-back of stock relief calculated as follows:-

1. Decrease in work-in-progress over the year (£105,000 – £70,000)	£35,000
2. Stock relief claimed in past years	75,000
Stock relief claw-back is the lower of 1. and 2.	£35,000

The income tax assessment on the firm for 1978/79 will finally be:-

Profit	£60,000
Add Stock relief claw-back	35,000
	95,000
Less Capital allowances	6,000
Tax payable on	£89,000

Claw-Back Explained

Example 8.2 is probably self-explanatory but to put the matter beyond doubt the rules are that the amount of claw-back is basically the decrease in work-in-progress over the year. But the amount clawed back cannot be more than the stock relief given in the past. In the above examples the past stock relief consisted of £25,000 for the year ending 31 December 1976 and £50,000 for previous years. Of course, the claw-back for the year ending 31 December 1977 reduces the past stock relief to £40,000 and this amount is then available to be clawed back in future years or, alternatively, to be augmented by further stock relief in future years.

On the other hand, there is one situation where it might be

thought that a claw-back ought to arise but in fact it does not. Suppose that, in example 8.2, the work-in-progress at 31 December 1977 was £107,000, that is, an increase of £2,000 over the year. If a stock relief calculation were prepared along the lines of that in example 8.1 it would reveal that the 15% deduction actually exceeded the work-in-progress increase. The result of this would be neutral: there would be no stock relief for 1977 but there would be no claw-back because the work-in-progress figure had not actually gone down over the year.

Stock Relief is given for Income Tax Years

Towards the end of chapter 4, under the heading "A separate partnership: a tax saving? — or a tax trap?" it was explained that tax depreciation allowances (capital allowances) are deducted from tax assessments *after* accounts years have been changed into income tax years, and the practical significance of this was briefly explained. Stock relief and claw-back follow the same form as capital allowances in this respect as can perhaps be seen from the examples in this chapter.

Stock Relief and Partnership Changes

In chapter 5 it was shown that where a new partner joins a partnership or an existing partner leaves there is, in general terms, a choice between treating the partnership as having closed and then re-opened or as having continued regardless of the change. The stock relief rules include provisions dealing with these situations. In simple terms, the rules provide that stock relief is unaffected if the partnership is treated as having continued. But if the partnership is treated as having closed and re-opened, then the past stock relief will be immediately clawed back unless the persons who were partners both before and after the change submit a notice of election to the Inspector of Taxes requesting that the partnership change should be ignored for the purposes of stock relief. This special notice of election must be sent to the Inspector of Taxes within two years of the date of the change in the partnership.

What of the Future?

For a long time the government did not commit themselves as to whether stock relief was going to be permanent or temporary. People therefore feared that relief given might be clawed back later even if stock levels did not fall, and some did not claim stock relief for that reason. The latest news about the government's intentions comes from the Chancellor of the Exchequer's Budget Speech on 11 April 1978. The position is as follows:

1. Stock relief will be continued indefinitely, and he hopes it will eventually be merged into a system of inflation accounting for tax purposes.

2. The 1979 Finance Bill will include provisions to make "un-clawbackable" the stock relief given in the first two years of the relief - in most cases this means stock relief given for the two accounts years ending next after 5 April 1973.

3. The 1979 Finance Bill will also include a general provision that any stock relief will become un-clawbackable six years after it is given.

Stock Relief — Some Practical Reminders

1. Stock relief is not given automatically; it must be claimed by the partnership and there is a time limit. To obtain stock relief for any particular accounting year, a claim must be made within two years after the end of the income tax year in which the accounting year closes. The stock relief in example 8.1 in respect of the year ending 31 December 1976 must be claimed by 5 April 1979. In practice, it is unlikely that the Inspector of Taxes will expect the partnership to submit a formal letter claiming the relief. The mere fact that the partnership's tax accountant calculates the relief when submitting the accounts will no doubt be regarded as a claim.
2. But, on the other hand, partnerships should not fall into the error of thinking that stock relief is compulsory. There will be some situations where, because of the future clawback, it will not be desirable to claim stock relief. For

example, a partnership would not want to claim stock relief for its accounting year ending 31 December 1976 if it knew that in its particular financial circumstances the relief was likely to be clawed back in the year ending 31 December 1977 and if the trend of profits was such that the rates of income tax payable on the 1977 profits were much higher than those payable on the 1976 profits. Before stock relief is claimed an attempt should be made to weigh the benefit of the relief against the future disadvantage of claw-back. Admittedly, there will be very many instances where the future disadvantage will not be capable of being quantified but in some marginal cases it may be worthwhile delaying the stock relief claim until towards the end of the time limit in order to have as much data as possible available before a decision is made.

3. It is almost certain that the law will be changed in 1979 so that the first two years' stock relief is made irrevocable. If so, partnerships should make sure that it is eliminated from their running totals of past stock relief, so that it is not accidentally clawed back.

CHAPTER NINE

OVERSEAS WORK

It's new!
In 1977 the Government brought in a tax relief for employees who spent some time working abroad. In 1978 they brought in a similar relief for partners and other self-employed people. The reason for these changes is apparently to encourage those at the "sharp end of the export drive". But the reliefs are given regardless of what work the person is doing abroad; he may be providing professional services, or importing for that matter.

The relief for partners and other self-employed people is probably best explained if we give an example first.

Example 9.1
Messrs John Johnson & Co are a firm of quantity surveyors based in the UK and Mr Jack Jackson is a partner in it. The firm makes up its accounts to 30 April in each year. Their profits for tax purposes for the year ending 30 April 1977, after deduction of capital allowances and stock relief, are £150,000. In the tax year ending 5 April 1979 Mr Jackson is entitled to a one-tenth share of the profits.

(It will not have escaped you – we hope! – that on the face of it Mr Jackson is liable to income tax for the tax year 1978/79 on one-tenth of £150,000, that is £15,000.)

But in the tax year ending 5 April 1979 Mr Jackson spends 40 days working abroad on the firm's business.

The result is that £411 of his £15,000 escapes tax altogether This is calculated as follows:

$$\frac{40}{365} \times £15{,}000 = £1{,}644$$

$$25\% \times £1{,}644 = £411$$

In other words one calculates on a time basis the amount of Mr Jackson's share of profits which is proportionate to his work abroad. One then takes 25% of that figure, and that 25% is entirely free of UK income tax. Mr Jackson is therefore only liable to tax for 1978/79 on £15,000 – £411 = £14,589.

All this does not sound very exciting, you may think. But if Mr Jackson is paying tax at a top rate of, say, 55% he is saving tax of 55% x £411 = £226. This is worth having.

Some important points

Some important points about the new rule are as follows:

1. The partner must do at least 30 days of work abroad in the tax year, otherwise he gets no relief at all. (The important question of what counts as a day of work abroad is explained below.)
2. There is no requirement that the days of work abroad must be continuous.
3. As many readers will have noticed, there is no connection of any kind between the profits on which relief is given and the work done abroad. In our example Mr Jackson spent forty days working abroad between 6 April 1978 and 5 April 1979 but the profits on which he got relief as a result were those of the year ending 30 April 1977. This is, of course, an oddity resulting from the preceding-year basis of assessment.
4. Employees, who get a similar relief as we have already said, do not have to work out their relief on a strict time basis. They can argue that a greater proportion of their salary is in fact attributable to work abroad than the time basis indicates and (if they can persuade their Inspector of Taxes of this) they will get relief

on that greater proportion of their salary. Self-employed people, partly because of the point explained at 3 above, do *not* have this right; their relief is always calculated on a time basis.

5. Employees get better treatment in another way too. If they work abroad for 365 days or more continuously (limited leave periods in the UK are allowed) they escape UK tax on their earnings altogether. The rule does not apply to self-employed people. For this reason it may be desirable for a partner who is posted abroad to step down and become an employee of his firm for the duration. This is something on which advice should be taken.
6. The relief must be claimed: it is not given automatically. It must be claimed within two years of the end of the tax year in question. In practice there is a special space for this in the partner's own tax return and he should send the Inspector with his return a note of his days of work abroad in the tax year.
7. The first year for which the new rule applies is the tax year 1978/79.

What is a Day of Work Abroad?

It is of course vital to know what constitutes a day of work abroad.

First of all, there is an overriding rule that a day cannot be a day of work abroad unless the partner is abroad at the end of it, that is at midnight. Day trips do not count. Partners should perhaps take the Night Ferry back from Paris or Brussels rather than flying back in the evening.

Subject to that, a day is a day of work abroad if it is a day spent abroad which is substantially devoted to his work: or a day which he spends in travelling abroad for the purposes of his work. But there is a relaxation for a partner who spends a continuous period overseas. If a partner spends at least seven consecutive days abroad and as a whole that period is substantially devoted to his work, then all the days in the continuous period count as days of work abroad.

These rules can best be illustrated by an example.

Example 9.2

Angela Walker is a partner in a firm of estate agents. She flies to the USA on business on Wednesday morning and arrives back in the UK at around lunchtime on Wednesday of the following week. She works on the Thursday, Friday, Monday and Tuesday, and rests on Saturday and Sunday. Her days of work abroad are seven, as follows:

Wednesday – day of travel	1
Thursday, Friday – actually working	2
Saturday, Sunday – allowable under 7-consecutive-days rule	2
Monday, Tuesday – actually working	2
Wednesday – fails overriding (midnight) test	0
Total	7

Maximising the Relief

Subject to commercial considerations a partner should maximise his days of work abroad. In particular, a person who would otherwise just fall short of the 30-day target should try to achieve it. One idea here flows from the fact that there is no requirement that the work done abroad must need to be done abroad. For example, a partner who would otherwise fall short of the 30-day target in a tax year by, say, two days, can stuff office papers into his briefcase, go to Dublin and spend two days working on them there.

A Major Overseas Project?

So far in this chapter we have talked about the new relief for overseas work brought in in 1978. This relief is all very well as far as it goes. But if a partnership is starting, or indeed if it already has, a major overseas activity of any kind, it may be able to do better than this. For example, a partnership may be planning to open a branch abroad, or it may be about to embark on a major assignment which is to be performed abroad, or may even buy a great deal of its materials abroad.

In circumstances like these the partners should consider setting up:

1. an overseas partnership, or

2. an overseas company

to handle the work.

It is outside the scope of this book to go further into this, and partners in this situation should take top-level tax advice: this will need to take exchange control and overseas tax into account as well as UK tax. But we want to say just one or two things about an overseas partnership. Provided that things are properly done, partners in a UK partnership can set up a quite separate partnership based overseas and they can be partners in it, even though they live in the UK. The profits of that overseas partnership will be liable to UK income tax in their hands, but only 75% of them; 25% of the profits will escape tax altogether. This is a quite different "25% exemption" from the one we talked about earlier; it is linked to the profits generated abroad rather than the partners' time spent abroad. (It is not possible unfortunately to get both reliefs on the same profits!) And it may also be possible to plan a tax-advantageous profit pattern in the overseas partnership in the sort of way discussed in Chapter 4 (though Chapter 4 cannot be applied exactly as it stands to an overseas partnership for various technical reasons). This is especially so where the overseas partnership is set up to handle a specific contract and will have a limited life-span. Again, top-level advice should be taken.

Exchange control permission must be obtained for setting up any partnership or company outside the Scheduled Territories (the Scheduled Territories being the United Kingdom, the Channel Islands, the Isle of Man, the Irish Republic and Gibraltar).

CHAPTER 9

ACTION POINTS

1 Claim the 30-day relief where you can. It is not given automatically.

2 Subject to overriding business considerations, maximise your days of work abroad. In particular, if you would otherwise fall just short of the 30-day target, you should take steps to achieve it.

3 If your partnership is planning, or has, a major overseas operation, look carefully at a more ambitious idea – setting up an overseas company or overseas partnership.

CHAPTER TEN

CALCULATING THE FIRM'S INCOME TAX LIABILITY; DIVIDING THE TAX BETWEEN THE PARTNERS; DATE OF PAYMENT OF TAX

Introduction

Until now, this book has concentrated on the way in which a partnership arrives at the amount of business profit assessable to tax for any particular income tax year, and has looked at a large number of detailed aspects of this problem. The time has now come to consider how the taxable profit is turned into an income tax liability and this will be done in this chapter, using the firm of Stan and Ollie introduced in chapter 1 for illustration. Calculating the income tax liability is largely an arithmetical process which produces no great opportunity for tax planning or tax saving and therefore the subject is considered in a relatively brief and simple form.

Dividing the Tax Assessment Between the Partners

If we return to the introductory sketch in chapter 1 we will see that at stage 2 of the summary for the firm of Stan and Ollie the profit for tax purposes for the year ending 30 June 1977 was £34,000. The detailed discussion in subsequent chapters has shown that this figure of £34,000 is more accurately described as the income tax assessment for the year 1978/79 (chapter 4) after deducting capital allowances and stock relief (chapters 6, 7 and 8). In calculating the income tax payable for 1978/79, the first step is to divide the amount of £34,000 between the two partners, Stan and Ollie. Readers may perhaps wonder why it is necessary to allocate this figure between the partners. There are two reasons which can most easily be understood after the calculations have been studied and which will, therefore, be explained a little later.

Calculating the Firm's Income Tax Liability

It will be remembered from chapter 1 that Stan and Ollie were each entitled to one-half of the profits. Some further personal information is now required before the firm's income tax liability can be worked out. In order to prevent the principles involved being overshadowed by excessive detail, the calculations will be kept very simple by assuming that the only personal tax reliefs to which Stan and Ollie are entitled are the married man's allowance in each case; and that Stan has allowable interest on his house-purchase of £900. (It is worth mentioning that had either of them had children under sixteen or in full-time education they would, in 1978/79, also receive tax allowances for them. But the non-taxable social security child benefits are being phased in and in consequence tax allowances for children are being abolished on 6 April 1979 except in the case of certain students and certain children resident overseas.)

The Stan & Ollie Partnership
Calculation of Income Tax payable for 1978-79

	Stan		Ollie		Total	
Income tax assessment for 1978-79 after deducting stock relief and capital allowances — ½ each partner		£17,000		£17,000		£34,000
Less: Married man's personal allowance	£1,535			1,535	£3,070	
interest	900	2,435		—	900	3,970
		14,565		15,465		30,030
Income tax payable:						
First £ 750 @ 25%	£ 750 @ 25%	187	£ 750 @ 25%	187	£1,500 @ 25%	375
Next 7,250 @ 33%	7,250 @ 33%	2,392	7,250 @ 33%	2,392	14,500 @ 33%	4,785
Next 1,000 @ 40%	1,000 @ 40%	400	1,000 @ 40%	400	2,000 @ 40%	800
Next 1,000 @ 45%	1,000 @ 45%	450	1,000 @ 45%	450	2,000 @ 45%	900
Next 1,000 @ 50%	1,000 @ 50%	500	1,000 @ 50%	500	2,000 @ 50%	1,000
Next 1,500 @ 55%	1,500 @ 55%	825	1,500 @ 55%	825	3,000 @ 55%	1,650
Next 1,500 @ 60%	1,500 @ 60%	900	1,500 @ 60%	900	3,000 @ 60%	1,800
Next 2,000 @ 65%	565 @ 65%	367	1,465 @ 65%	952	2,030 @ 65%	1,319
Next 2,500 @ 70%	—	—	—	—	—	—
Next 5,500 @ 75%	—	—	—	—	—	—
Remainder @ 83%	—	—	—	—	—	—
	14,565	6,022	15,465	6,607	30,030	12,629

It is assumed that neither Stan nor Ollie worked overseas for 30 days or more in the year; if either of them had then his £17,000 would have been treated as reduced and his tax computation would have been done on the lower figure, as explained in Chapter 9.

For simplicity odd pence have been left off tax figures in the table. The odd pence would not be ignored in practice though and the Inland Revenue would issue demands on the firm for exactly £12,629.50. The income tax calculations issued to the Stan and Ollie partnership by the Inland Revenue would, incidentally, show only the details set out in the total column above; the individual partner details would usually be sent by the Inland Revenue to the respective partners. The firm would, in due course, pay the income tax of £12,629.50 and in the partnership books of account this payment would be charged to Stan and Ollie respectively in the sums of £6,022.25 and £6,607.25. It is now possible to appreciate the two reasons why the figure of £34,000 has first to be divided between the partners. First, it is not possible to determine the appropriate rates of tax until the income has been allocated between the partners. Second, for internal bookkeeping purposes, the partnership will need to know how much of the total tax to charge to each of the partners.

The two-partner structure of the Stan and Ollie partnership is a simple one but the principles described above will be equally applicable no matter how many partners there are in the firm.

Income Tax Rates for 1978/79

The figures shown in the calculations above indicate the rates of tax payable on earned income. Additionally to this, there is a further tax on investment income (for example, dividends, interest received, rents received, etc); the rate varies according to the amount of investment income in the particular tax year but is at a maximum of 15%. The overall effect of all this is, of course, that the maximum rate of income tax for 1978/79 is 98% on investment income. Readers who are interested in tax terminology will like to know that the rate of income tax applied to the first band of income (25%) is known as the lower rate, the rate for the next band (33%) is known as the basic rate and the subsequent rates (40% to 83%) are called the higher rates. The further tax charged on investment income (maximum 15%) is usually referred to as the investment income surcharge but this description will not, in fact, be found in the tax statutes – there, the tax is described as income tax at the additional rate.

Changes in the Partners' Profit-Shares

In the introduction to chapter 4, it was explained that the tax rules, having transformed the year ending 30 June 1977 to the year ending 5 April 1979, then treat the business profit from July 1976 to June 1977 just as if it had actually been earned in the year to 5 April 1979. This tax fiction can affect the above explanation of the calculation of a firm's income tax liability.

Suppose that in the Stan and Ollie partnership, the two partners shared profits equally in the year ending 30 June 1977 but from 1 July 1977 onwards the profit-shares were changed, because Ollie went into semi-retirement, to Stan 80% and Ollie 20%. The figure of £34,000 is treated for tax purposes as if it had been earned in the year 1978/79 and it must therefore be divided between the partners in their new profit-share ratios of 80% and 20%. The fact that the amount of £34,000 has been derived from the partnershp accounts for the year ending 30 June 1977 when profits were shared equally is totally irrelevant.

In these circumstances, the calculations set out earlier would not be applicable. The column headed "Stan" would start with an amount of £27,200 (80% of £34,000) and the column headed "Ollie" would start with £6,800 (20%). This would, of course, produce a tax liability on the firm of an amount different from £12,629.50 and would considerably alter the allocation of the total liability between the two partners. Ollie's share of the total tax liability for 1978/79 would be quite modest if it were compared with the half share of the profits for the year ending 30 June 1977 which he has obtained.

It can be seen that changes in the profit shares of individual partners can produce peculiar and unfair results as between the partners, especially when the changes are violent or where the firm's profit fluctuates considerably from one year to another. It can also be seen that the rule requiring the division to be carried out according to the profit shares in the income tax year rather than the accounting year can cause considerable delay in calculating the firm's ultimate tax liability; in practice, provisional calculations are often agreed with the Inland Revenue in such circumstances and they are adjusted at a later time.

Other Factors affecting the Division between the Partners

In most partnerships of any size, there are further arithmetical factors that need to be taken into account in making the division between the partners, notably, salaries paid to "full" partners and interest on partners' capital. Towards the end of chapter 3, it was pointed out that such amounts are not allowed as a deduction against profits for tax purposes. Their only relevance in the tax field is that they will be brought in as one of the arithmetical factors in dividing the taxable profit between the partners. If the Stan and Ollie partnership paid salaries to partners or interest on capital then the amount of salary and interest paid away for *the year ending 5 April 1979* will be used as one of the factors in allocating the amount of £34,000. This again will cause delay in agreeing the firm's ultimate tax bill and it may be that the firm and the Inspector of Taxes will agree to reduce the delay a little by using the interest and salary figures for the year ending 30 June 1978 (not 1977) in dividing up the amount of £34,000 for 1978/79.

When does the Tax have to be Paid?

The normal rule is that the firm's income tax is payable in two equal instalments. Returning to the firm of Stan and Ollie, one-half of the 1978/79 tax (£6,314.75) falls due on 1 January 1979 and the other half on 1 July 1979. The rule is that the first half of the tax liability is due for payment on 1 January in the income tax year concerned and the second half six months later. This normal rule covers the case where the firm does not have any investment income. If, though, the total tax bill includes any tax on investment income (for example, the firm might have used some of its surplus cash to buy a piece of property purely to derive the rental income from it) then the tax on the investment income is payable in one amount on 1 January in the income tax year concerned.

All of this assumes, of course, that the tax bill is agreed in good time. If there is delay in agreeing the firm's income tax position the due dates mentioned earlier may not be completely applicable.

National Insurance Contributions

A discussion of the scheme of national insurance contributions is outside the scope of this book but it is appropriate to make a brief mention of class 4 contributions if only because they are collected along with the firm's income tax. Class 4 contributions are payable by self-employed people in addition to the flat-rate weekly contribution (class 2). The class 4 contribution for each partner is calculated on a percentage basis by reference to his share of the firm's taxable profits, after deducting capital allowances and stock relief but before deducting overseas work relief. The method of calculation is to take the band of profits between £2,250 and £7,000 for each partner for the particular income tax year and charge 5% on this band. (The figures were different before 6 April 1979). When the Stan and Ollie partnership receive their income tax demands they will find a figure of Class 4 national insurance contributions added to the income tax of £12,629.50.

CHAPTER ELEVEN

WOULD YOU BE BETTER OFF WITH A COMPANY?

How this Chapter is Structured

Almost all partnerships have, at one time or another, given thought to the question whether they would be better off if they ran their partnerships side by side with a company, perhaps a limited company or an unlimited company (the full significance of these terms will be explained shortly). Some partnerships have even toyed with the idea of converting the whole of their operation into a company structure.

Because there is no simple general solution to the question whether a company organisation will produce tax advantages this chapter will initially examine the way in which companies are taxed and will make comparisons from time to time with the method of taxing partnerships. This will lead to an outline examination of the question whether readers should or should not have a company.

The chapter then turns to those readers who ought to have a company, or who already have one, and considers what they should be doing with the company to maximise the tax benefits flowing from it. Finally, there is a review of some of the large number of practical problems and opportunities created by the use of a company together with some routine reminders. The subject is dealt with quite deliberately at some length and if an excuse is needed for this in a book entitled Partnership Taxation it is that the authors' practical experience in the field of advising partnerships shows that the use of companies is an area on which assistance is often sought, and because there is so little in the way of useful written material which can be used as practical guidance.

The chapter is largely directed toward the professional partnership rather than the trading or manufacturing partnership since, whereas the latter can usually relatively easily turn themselves into limited companies if they wish, there are often professional reasons why practices cannot make the move so easily. Nevertheless, much of this chapter can usefully be applied to a trading or manufacturing partnership which wishes to obtain the tax benefits that are sometimes available from running a parallel limited company or wishes to consider whether it should be entirely converted to a limited company.

Before we plunge into an examination of the scheme of company tax, a few paragraphs are needed to explain some of the terminology.

Limited Companies and Unlimited Companies

Readers will all be fully familiar with the concept of a limited company and the majority will be aware of the major legal differences between a limited company and a partnership. They are, of course, many and varied but for the purposes of the present discussion only two need be mentioned: firstly, a person making a claim against a partnership can normally, if the partnership's funds are insufficient, have recourse to the private assets of the partners whereas, in general, in the case of a limited company shareholders cannot be required to dip into their own pockets to meet claims against the company; second, partnerships are liable to income tax whereas limited companies pay corporation tax under a very different system.

A special form of beast somewhere between the partnership and the limited company is an unlimited company. This is formed under provisions in the Companies Acts which are of course the statutes which regulate all companies. An unlimited company does not afford to the shareholders the protection of a limited company since claims can be traced through the company to them individually; in this respect it is very much like a partnership. But for tax purposes it is treated in virtually the same way as a limited company. Unlimited companies are not (for obvious reasons) used very much by trading and manufacturing concerns but it is often the case that if a professional practice wishes to create a company it can, under the rules of its profession, use only the unlimited and not the limited form. Because this chapter is concerned not with the question of creditors pursuing the shareholders but with tax, and because the tax provisions for both unlimited and limited companies are largely the same, the expression "company" will in general be used in this chapter to denote either form of company. It is often found that in common parlance a partnership business is referred to as a company but this is a technically wrong description and in this chapter the word "company" and the word "partnership" will be used as mutually exclusive terms.

Service Company

This expression is not a term of legal art. The phrase will not be found in the Companies Acts or in the tax statutes. The words "service company" are however in wide general use to describe a company that provides services to a partnership. For example, a partnership might have a staff of 50, it might run six business motor cars, own a small computer and some expensive printing equipment. The partnership could form a company and the 50 staff members could be moved off the payroll of the partnership and onto that of the company. In a rather similar way, the company could become the owner of the motor cars, the computer and the printing machinery. The partnership would use all of the facilities now owned by the company (and which previously it had owned itself) and would pay the company a service charge which could be calculated from the cost of the facilities plus, say, an uplift of 7½%. (More about the important question of the mechanics of the uplift later in this chapter under the heading "What should we do with our service company?").

There could be a variety of commercial reasons for creating the type of service company just described but, in practice, it is often the case that a prime function of the service company is to cream off some of the profits of the partnership in the hope that they will be taxed more leniently in the company. Once again, more about this later in this chapter. Now we can move to our examination of the company tax system.

The "Imputation" Tax System

Many readers will know that the method that has been used in this country since 1973 for taxing companies is entitled the imputation system. The first thing to do in trying to understand this system if to forget its title! The word "imputation" is frightening and, at this stage, does nothing to assist an understanding of the way the system works.

The basic rule is that, apart from some exceptional situations outside the scope of this discussion, companies are unlike partnerships in that they do not pay income tax on their income. Instead companies pay corporation tax on their profits and the first problem that we have to face is discovering the rate of corporation tax. Most company financial executives think that they know the rate of tax on their company's current profits, but they do not. The rate is fixed by the government annually in arrear and the latest rate to be announced was for the year to 31 March 1979, 52%. (For some companies a reduced rate of only 42% is charged – this is discussed later in this chapter.) The two rates were announced by the Chancellor of the Exchequer in the Budget on 3 April 1979 – and even these rates may be changed in the second budget we have been promised after the general election. The rates for the year ending 31 March 1980 will not be known until the Spring of 1980 and may well differ from 52% and 42%. But, for convenience of illustration, the present and future rate is usually taken as 52% in this chapter.

Using this rate of 52%, the structure of company taxation in a typical case could be expressed as follows:-

Profit (not the profit shown by the company's accounts but the adjusted figure as adopted for tax purposes)	£100,000
Corporation tax @ 52%	52,000
Profit after tax	£48,000

And if the company pays a dividend to its shareholders the figures could be continued:

Profit after tax	£48,000
Dividend – actual amount paid to shareholders	40,000
Profit after tax and dividend payment	£8,000

Dividends paid to Shareholders

Some readers will be concerned about the treatment of the dividend payment in the above figures. This is because it is still fresh in the minds of many people that there was a time not so very long ago when companies declared a dividend and then deducted tax before paying it to their shareholders, so that there was a "gross" dividend and a "net" dividend. Perhaps you are asking yourself at this moment whether the amount of £40,000 shown above is "gross" or "net". Strictly speaking, it is neither. The system of deducting tax from dividends was abandoned in 1973 and in the case above the company will have declared a dividend of £40,000 and will actually pay that amount to its shareholders.

But you may well wonder about the personal tax position of the shareholders who receive the dividend of £40,000. Here we come to what is indeed the core of the present system of company taxation. To understand this feature of the system one needs to be reminded that in the previous chapter it was mentioned that the basic rate of personal income tax is 33%. The rule with regard to dividends is that when the shareholders receive their dividend they are deemed to have already paid tax at the basic rate on the dividend even though they have not actually done so!

A bit of arithmetical juggling will show that with a rate of 33% the shareholders who receive dividends totalling £40,000 are deemed notionally to have already paid income tax of £19,701. Of course, £19,701 is not 33% of £40,000. But consider the following:

Actual dividend paid	£40,000
Notional income tax deemed to have been paid on dividend at 33%	£19,701
Dividend plus notional tax	£59,701

The notional tax of £19,701 is 33% of £59,701. It is what you might describe as circular arithmetic but it makes sense within the concept of the system of company tax.

Strangely enough the Inland Revenue will regard the shareholders in the company just as if they had actually paid income tax of £19,701 and these shareholders will be credited with this amount of tax by the Inland Revenue when their personal tax is calculated. For example, if a particular shareholder has a personal top rate of income tax on investment income of 60% he will be credited with 33% and will pay tax on the dividend only at the net rate of 27%. (The 27% will naturally enough be calculated on the amount of the dividend plus the income tax already regarded as paid). Conversely, if a shareholder is not personally liable to income tax at all he can obtain a cheque from the Inland Revenue for the income tax he has notionally paid.

The question may be posed: if the Inland Revenue are prepared to credit shareholders with total income tax amounting to £19,701 which they have not paid, then who has actually paid this to the Inland Revenue? The answer is really quite simple: the company has paid the tax. In effect, the Inland Revenue looks at the £52,000 corporation tax which was paid by the company and attributes £19,701 of it to the shareholders as if they had actually paid it themselves. This attribution of part of the company's tax payment to the shareholders is a central feature of the system of company tax and if you are interested in semantics you will know that another word for "attribution" is "imputation". Which is almost where we came in!

"Tax Credit"

The final polish can be given to the discussion above by getting the terminology correct. Looking at the dividend paid to shareholders, the amount of £19,701 which has been described as notional income tax is, properly speaking, referred to as "tax credit". The amount of £59,701 which is the actual dividend plus the tax credit has, unfortunately, no official phrase to describe it. It is sometimes called "effective gross" or something similar but this is an unfortunate description in some ways since it tends to carry the idea that something is deducted from a dividend which is not now true.

Certainly the words "gross" and "net" should never be used.

The Total Tax Effect

It is instructive to pause at this stage to consider the overall impact of tax on a company and its shareholders. The rate of corporation tax on company profits is relatively modest when it is compared with the top rate of income tax on partnership business profits – 83%, as was explained in chapter 10. But unfortunately the payment of corporation tax does not bring an end to the total tax burden on the company and its shareholders.

If the company pays a dividend, the shareholders will pay further personal income tax on the dividend depending upon their individual tax rates. The top rate of income tax on dividend income and other forms of investment income is 98%. Bearing in mind that the shareholder is given a credit for notional tax on the dividend at 33%, there could be as much as 65% personal income tax to be paid when a shareholder receives a dividend from the company. Which is, of course, additional to the corporation tax already paid by the company.

And what if the company wishes to reduce the personal income tax on its shareholders by not paying a dividend? There are some instances, which will be explored later in this chapter, where the company will not in practice be able to resist the payment of a dividend. But, ignoring these cases for the moment, if the company does not pay a dividend then the *immediate* total tax burden is limited to the relatively modest rate of corporation tax and no more. There is though a *future* tax burden to be borne in mind. Because the company is ploughing back its profits rather than paying dividends, the assets of the company will be increasing in amount year by year. The result of this is that the value of the shares in the company will also increase as time goes by. The shareholders in the company will therefore be holding an asset (the shares) which will be moving up in value because of the ploughing back of profits by the company. Now, anyone who holds an asset that is increasing in value must face the possibility of capital gains tax at some future time. For example, suppose that you and your five partners hold shares in a service company and that in 1979 the profit in the service company after corporation tax amounts to £30,000 and this is ploughed back into the company rather than used for the payment of dividends. If, in 1995, you sell your personal holding in the service company (perhaps because you have retired from the partnership) then the sale proceeds will indirectly reflect your share of the £30,000 ploughed back in 1979 (and. of course, amounts of a similar nature for other years) and this will become liable to capital gains tax. At the present time, capital gains tax is at the maximum rate of 30% but in the circumstances just outlined it will be charged at the rate applicable in 1995 and you will need a very efficient crystal ball in 1979 to estimate the rate then.

If, then, the company does not pay dividends it is easy to form a mistaken view that the total tax burden is no more than corporation tax. Strictly speaking, some account needs to be taken of future capital gains tax. In broad terms, capital gains tax will become payable when shares in the company are either sold or given away during lifetime or if the company is liquidated. But, because this is usually so far into the future and at an unpredictable rate of tax many readers will choose to discount the future capital gains tax down to a fairly modest sum at present-day values. In this connection, it is also worth remembering that if the shares are held until death capital gains tax is not charged on the appreciation in value up to the date of death.

In summary, the total tax effect on the company and its shareholders will vary according to whether dividends are paid. To the extent that dividends are paid away the total tax burden is an immediate corporation tax charge plus an immediate personal income tax charge. To the extent that profits are ploughed back the tax burden is an immediate corporation tax charge plus a possible future personal capital gains tax charge.

Reduced Rates of Corporation Tax

In the discussion so far, a corporation tax rate of 52% has been used. But "small companies" are not chargeable at the full rate. Instead, a special reduced "small company" rate is applied.

The reader no doubt visualises a "small company" as a company with little assets and few employees. But the normal business concept of a "small company" has no relevance for tax purposes. A "small company" (for tax purposes only) is a company with profits below £85,000 in any particular year.

It will be recalled from the discussion earlier in this chapter that the full rate of corporation tax for the year to 31 March 1979 is (provisionally) 52% and that the rate for subsequent periods is not yet known. The small company rate is (provisionally) 42% for the year to 31 March 1979 and similarly is not yet known for later periods.

The *full* benefit of the lower 42% rate will apply only to those companies with profits of £50,000 and below. For those companies with profits between £50,000 and £85,000 the overall rate of corporation tax gradually increases from 42% to 52%. When profits reach the £85,000 threshold the full rate of 52% bites.

As can perhaps be expected, in measuring the company's profits in order to determine whether it is entitled to the lower small companies rate, one looks not at the profits shown in the company's accounts but (and this may be a vastly different figure) the profit as adjusted for tax purposes and after deducting capital allowances and stock relief.

Where a company has one or more associated companies, then the threshold figures given above (the figures of £50,000 and £85,000) are substantially lower in the case of each company. This rule was made to stop tax avoidance by setting up more than one company, but it applies even though there may have been no intention to avoid tax. The sort of thing that sometimes happens is that two friends together set up a company to run a business, one of them having a majority interest. It turns out later that that man has a small property-dealing company which counts as an associated company, and as a result the corporation tax position – of both companies – is not so good as had been thought.

No Preceding-year Basis

Chapter 4 explained the problems facing partnerships in relating accounts years to income tax years and how this has created what is normally known as the preceding-year basis.

None of this applies to companies. Companies are assessed to corporation tax by reference to their own accounting years: a company preparing a set of business accounts for the year ending 30 June 1978, for example, will receive a corporation tax assessment for that accounting year and not for the arbitrary income tax year ending 5 April. When the rate of corporation tax changes, the new rate comes into effect on 1 April in any particular year so that companies often have to apportion their business profits to periods before and after 1 April in calculating the amount of tax they have to pay.

Because the complex rules for turning accounting years into income tax years have no application to companies, companies have the advantage of not having to worry about the pitfalls explained in chapter 4 and demonstrated in case history 4.3. Conversely, they have the disadvantage of not having the tax saving opportunities shown in the modified version of case history 4.3.

Date of Payment of Corporation Tax

Here again, the rules are very different from those applying to partnerships. In chapter 10, it was shown that the income tax on the profits of the Stan and Ollie partnership for the year ending 30 June 1977 falls due for payment in January 1979 and July 1979. For companies, the rules are much more complex and only a brief outline explanation is appropriate in this book.

Suppose that one is considering the corporation tax bill on a company for its accounting year ending 30 June 1977. Usually, the tax will in effect be paid in instalments. Firstly, a portion of the corporation tax bill will become due to the Inland Revenue around about the time that the company pays a dividend or dividends in the year ending 30 June 1977. The company will not be aware of its final corporation tax liability at that point of time because it will not yet have prepared its business accounts. Therefore, this payment in advance of the year-end is measured as a fraction of the amount of the dividend: it is called advance corporation tax. Some time after 30 June 1977 when the company's accounts for the year have been completed, the correct amount of corporation tax will be calculated, the advance corporation tax already paid will be deducted and the balance will then be payable to the Inland Revenue. Precisely at what time the balance of tax will be payable to the Inland Revenue depends upon how long ago the company first started to function. Sufficient for present purposes to say that the company will not have the extended period available to the Stan and Ollie partnership where the payment of the income tax on the profits for the year ending 30 June 1977 was extended as far as July 1979.

In a nutshell, companies are usually worse off than partnerships so far as concerns the length of the period from the date they earn their profits until the tax falls due.

Can we make an Overall Comparison of Companies and Partnerships?

Possibly, while you have been reading this outline of the company tax system you have had one eye on the way in which your partnership is taxed so that you can develop a view as to whether a service company would create tax benefits for your firm. If you have been trying to make this comparison, you may have noted that this is bedevilled by one arithmetical feature. What exactly is the total impact of the tax burden on a company and its shareholders? Corporation tax is at 42% or 52%. Capital gains tax on ploughed-back profits can perhaps be discounted to a minimal figure. But what do you bring into the calculation in respect of the personal income tax paid by the shareholders on dividends that they receive from the company? Is this not a variable figure depending upon how much the company will want to pay away in dividends? Will not the company in practice deliberately keep down the level of dividends in order to limit the total tax burden? Or do the Inland Revenue have a trump card up their sleeve which they can use if the company attempts this? The answer is that there is legislation under which the Inland Revenue do have certain powers to force the payment of dividends; but recently Parliament has eased the law, and the result is that the ordinary service company, and indeed the ordinary small company of any kind, is not affected by these powers.

Shortfall

Let us explain a little about the powers of the Inland Revenue to require dividend payments. They are usually called "shortfall" powers (the company has *fallen short* of paying what is considered to be the proper dividend) or "apportionment" powers (the Inland Revenue *apportions* part of the company's profits between its shareholders).

To begin with, the Inland Revenue only has these powers in the case of a "close" company. What is a "close" company? It is not practicable to plunge here into an explanation of exactly what companies are and what companies are not close. The general idea is that a close company is a company under the control of only a comparatively small number of shareholders. It is difficult for a company which is not quoted on the Stock Exchange to avoid being a close company.

The basic shortfall rule can probably best be explained with the help of an example.

Example 11.2
Z Limited is a close company engaged in manufacturing. For its accounting year ending on 31 December 1978 it has profits for tax purposes, after deducting capital allowances and stock relief, of £180,000. It pays a dividend for the year, voluntarily, of £20,000.

Profits for tax purposes	£180,000
Less corporation tax @ 52%	93,600
After-tax profit	86,400
50% of £86,400	43,200
Less dividend actually paid	20,000
"Apportionable profit"	23,200

You find the company's after-tax profit for the accounting year in question. You take 50% of that and deduct any dividend paid voluntarily. What is left is the apportionable profit. Subject to what we say below, Z Limited must either distribute the £23,200 as additional dividend; or Z Limited can keep the money, but in that case it must pay itself the higher rate income tax and investment income surcharge that the shareholders would have had to pay had it been distributed.

However, there is an escape route from shortfall. Z Limited can avoid this shortfall liability if it can convince its Inspector of Taxes that it needs to plough back the £23,200 into the business. Perhaps it needs the money to expand its office premises, or to survive the effects of inflation on stock prices, or it may need to put the money aside to buy a computer. But the company has got to show that its other cash resources are insufficient: for example, the Inspector would expect the other 50% of the profits – the £43,200 which does *not* enter into the calculation above – to be ploughed back into the business before he would relent on the £23,200.

Shortfall – "Abatement" Relief

We said above that in practice shortfall will not apply to the ordinary service company, or to the ordinary small company of any kind. This is because of what is called "abatement" relief. We do not go into the arithmetic of this here, but its effect is that

1. A company which has profits of £45,402 or less in the year in question before corporation tax can have no shortfall liability at all.

2. The full rigour of the shortfall rules (as explained in Example 11.2) only applies to a company which has profits of £156,250 or more in the year in question before corporation tax.

The profit figures referred to are profits for tax purposes after deduction of capital allowances and stock relief. These often reduce profits very considerably. Furthermore, in the case of a service company, it is usually prudent for quite separate reasons not to try to route too much profit into the company: this is discussed below. So it is very unlikely that, except in the case of the very largest partnerships, the service company will be making a net profit of more than £45,402 per annum. Except in rare cases shortfall is not going to worry a professional partnership with a service company.

Before we leave the subject of abatement relief, we must make one point that is easily forgotten. This is that where a company has one or more associated companies, then the figures at which shortfall bites are substantially lower in the case of each company. This is a very similar rule to the one which applies in connexion with the reduced rate of corporation tax. Readers should not set up a company without considering whether there is any other company in existence which would be an "associated company" and looking at what the effect on shortfall liability would be.

Should we have a Company?

The explanation of the principal features of the company tax system has been completed and readers will now appreciate why there is no generalised and simple solution to the question whether a partnership should create a service company, or in appropriate cases, turn itself entirely into a company. Larger partnerships will probably need to take specialised advice on the question and it is hoped that the explanations in this chapter will assist them in recognising the point of time at which such advice is needed. Partnerships of more modest size may be able to form a view on the question whether they would be better off with a company by considering the information in this chapter in comparison with the rates of income tax they pay on their particular partnership profits.

A long-term comparison of after-tax income with and without a company is bound to involve a fair amount of crystal ball gazing. In over-simplified form the comparison might, in a particular case, look something like this (the comparative amounts and percentages would vary from one case to another):

Profit creamed off into company over next 10 years	£200,000
Less corporation tax — crystal ball indicates an average rate of 45%	90,000
Carried forward	110,000

Brought forward	£110,000
No dividends and no shortfall liability.	
Possible future capital gains tax on shareholders – crystal ball suggests 10% covers the risk	11,000
After-tax income	£99,000
But if the profit were in the partnership	£200,000
Income tax would be paid at partners' rates – crystal ball reveals a rate of 60% on average	120,000
After-tax income	£80,000

Company Taxation – the Major Features Summarised
Because of the far-ranging scope of the discussion so far in this chapter, it will probably be helpful if at this stage the features of company taxation already explained are briefly signposted. Assuming, as will probably be the case, that the company in mind is a close company, the principal features are:

1. Corporation tax is at 52%, reducing to 42% for small or medium-sized profits.

2. Shareholders will be liable to tax on dividends. But they will be credited with tax at the basic rate of 33%.

3. To the extent that profits are ploughed back , a possible capital gains tax charge on the shareholders is being built up for the future.

4. Unlike partnerships, there is no preceding-year basis.

5. The time-lag between the end of an accounting year and the due date for paying tax is usually shorter for a company than a partnership.

6. The Inland Revenue have certain powers to force payment of dividends: but these powers are unlikely to affect service companies, and many other small companies.

What shall we do with our Service Company?

Assuming that a decision has been taken to have a company, what should be done to maximise the tax benefits? Obviously there is little point in having created a company in order to get the benefit of lower rates of tax if so little profit is generated in the company that the tax saving is hardly worth the exercise. In reviewing the tax strategy of a number of professional firms, we have sometimes found that partnerships have created service companies and then have used them to such a limited extent that only a dribble of profit arises in the company with little or no ultimate tax saving.

The problem does not arise in the relatively rare instances where the whole of the partnership activity can be converted into a company. But where a service company has been created, consideration needs to be given to the question of getting a worthwhile amount of profit into the company. The profit will usually go over in the form of percentage uplift which the service company applies to its costs when billing them to the partnership. However, a partnership cannot simply push what profit it likes into the service company by getting the company to fix its fee appropriately. The fee the partnership pays the service company has got to be wholly and exclusively expended for the purpose of the partnership's business (this rule was discussed in Chapter 3), otherwise it will not be an allowable deduction in the partnership's own income tax computation and the last state will be worse than the first. The "wholly and exclusively" rule means in this context that the fee must be a commercially reasonable one for the services which the service company provides.

The Inland Revenue are currently taking a tough line on this, and are querying any uplift of more than 7½%. They say that this is a reasonable mark-up for a company which takes no risks and in effect simply passes on orders from the partnership. Our view is that the Inland Revenue are being unrealistic. Outside bodies often provide businesses with the same sort of services as a service company does, and take no great risks – for example it is common to contract with an agency that the agency should provide the services of staff on a continuing basis – and those bodies charge an uplift of more than 7½%.

Nevertheless as things stand our advice is as follows. The partnership must decide whether it wants its service company's mark-up to be more than 7½% or not. If they do not, then there is no problem. If they do, then the role and operation of the service company must be carefully thought out in advance so that it operates so far as possible like an independent commercial entity and runs some risk of loss. This will certainly mean taking advice.

Those who are faced with this tricky question of an acceptable uplift will find it useful to consider the practical case history that follows which is based on a reported court case. Although it is not claimed that anything startlingly positive arises from the case, it has some helpful features and in some respects it provides a clue or two as to how things should not be done.

Case History 11.2

This case deals with the question whether a firm of chartered accountants were entitled to deduct from their profits the charges paid by them to their service company. The case history is a simplified version of an actual court hearing in 1967.

The accounting firm of Payne, Stone, Fraser & Co utilised a service company called Bedford Row Nominees Ltd. The service company provided staff and other facilities for the partnership. The directors and shareholders of the service company were the same individuals as the partners in the firm.

It was decided that the service company would submit a statement of its total charges to the partnership only once every year and that the policy of the service company should be that it would not make an undue profit at the expense of the partnership.

Sometime in the summer of 1962 an agreement was reached with regard to the charges to be paid to the service company for the year ending 30 November 1961. This was an oral agreement made between the partners of the partnership on the one hand and the directors of the service company on the other hand. Under the agreement it was provided that the partnership should pay the service company £47,000 for the services provided in the year ending 30 November 1961.

At the time when the sum of £47,000 was agreed it was known that the total expenditure by the service company on salaries, lighting, heating, etc for the year ending 30 November 1961 was only £32,000 so that there was an uplift of £15,000. The facts in the case showed that the figure of £47,000 was reached on the understanding that the charge made by the service company for later years would be adjusted so as to secure for the service company a nominal profit only over the long term.

At a later time the charge to be made by the service company for the next year (the year ending 30 November 1962) was agreed between the partnership and the company. The amount was £21,000 and this took into account the "excess payment" in the previous year.

The reason for the "loading" of the charge for the year ending 30 November 1961 and the reversal of the "loading" in the following year was that this gave the partnership a profit pattern which was advantageous for income tax purposes. (Readers are reminded of the discussion of tax-advantageous profit patterns in the latter part of chapter 4). The Inspector of Taxes refused to allow the payment of £47,000 against the partnership's profits for the year ending 30 November 1961 and the case came before the Appeal Commissioners, that is, the independent tribunal whose task it is to hear tax disputes.

Among the facts which the Appeal Commissioners recorded as having been admitted or proved before them was the following:

> "From the point of view of the company £47,000 was a commercially reasonable price for the company to charge anybody for services costing £32,000. The firm got value for the £47,000 in the long term".

The Appeal Commissioners decided that the amount of

£47,000 paid by the partnership did not fall foul of the "wholly and exclusively" test and the amount should be allowed against the firm's profits for the year ending 30 November 1961.

......an oral agreement made between the partners of the partnership on the one hand and the directors of the service company on the other hand......

The Inland Revenue took the case further to the High Court where the partnership lost its argument. But, perhaps surprisingly, it was not the "wholly and exclusively" test that caused this defeat. To understand the decision in the case, readers will need to refresh themselves about the fundamental rule described in chapter 2. It was there stated that for income tax purposes, profits are initially to be calculated on ordinary commercial principles of accountancy. In the particular case now under review, the Court decided that ordinary commercial principles of accountancy, rather than the "wholly and exclusively" test, prevented the deduction of the full £47,000. As was said in the judgement in the case:

> "The attribution of any given outgoing to one or other period of account ....is a matter to be determined

> upon the ordinary principles of commercial accountancy. .... The partners .... arranged that .... the service company should add £15,000 to the actual cost of the services rendered in the year of account ended 30 November 1961 and make a corresponding deduction in making its service charges in the subsequent year or years of account. .... This misattribution is manifestly contrary to the ordinary principles of commercial accountancy ..... "

The Court reversed the decision of the Appeal Commissioners and allowed the partnership to deduct in its accounts for the year ending 30 November 1961 only £32,000 plus a nominal figure of profit for the service company. (The Court did not indicate what was to happen to the charges paid to the service company for the year ending 30 November 1962. It is outside the scope of this practical guide to discuss the technically interesting arguments and counter-arguments that could be put forward with regard to the allowance in the second year and, regrettably, readers must be left to conjecture on this point.)

There are at least two points of practical significance in this case history. First, it was not simply the addition of the uplift of £15,000 which caused defeat for the partnership. It was the fact that the partners also arranged that a deduction of £15,000 should be made in subsequent years. Second, it is instructive that the Appeal Commissioners regarded the amount of £47,000 as a commercially reasonable price, from the point of view of the service company, for it to charge. But readers must bear in mind the Inland Revenue's present attitude to service company mark-ups as well.

Companies — Some Other Things to do with Them

Maximising the uplift used for a service company may well produce tax advantages in many instances but there are other courses of action open to partnerships contemplating service companies. It is not feasible to discuss all the possibilities in a book of this character and, in any event, most partnerships embarking on major sophisticated tax planning would need detailed and highly specialised advice to cover their own particular circumstances. But a few possibilities can be touched upon briefly:

(a) A company could be formed to become a partner in the firm. The company would receive a share of profits in much the same way as any other partner. This might permit a greater sum to be paid out of the partnership to the company than is possible if the company simply provided services with a percentage uplift.

(b) The partners will probably be directors of the service company and it is open to them to draw directors' fees or other remuneration from it. Ordinarily the partners will not want to do so: in general the purpose of having the service company is to roll profit up, and if partners want income in their hands they will take it in the form of partnership profits. But there are two cases where they may want remuneration from the partnership.

1. Where the remuneration is in the form of tax-efficient benefits in kind — many of these are open to directors or employees but not to partners as such.

2. To qualify the partners for retirement benefits under an approved pension scheme (this is discussed at (3) below).

BUT the Inland Revenue are currently taking a tough line on how much of this remuneration is an allowable expense as far as the company's corporation tax is concerned. They are saying that in the circumstances of a service company running alongside a partnership only a few hundred pounds a year for each director is justifiable. This view is almost certainly wrong at least in the case where the director-partner spends a lot of his time on administrative work and it is clear that he is working for the service company when he does this work; but it does mean that some careful planning must be done where it is desired that a director-partner should draw significant remuneration from the company.

(c) A company that has, over the years, built up substantial cash assets may wish to distribute those assets to its shareholders. In broad terms, the most tax-advantageous course to follow would be to liquidate the company. But advice should be taken by reference to the particular circumstances, before such a course of action is implemented on the question whether the Inland Revenue could successfully apply the special anti-avoidance rules regarding transactions in company shares contained in Section 460 Income and Corporation Taxes Act 1970.

(d) Some professional partnerships may use the company tax rules to their advantage by turning their entire professional activity into a company; for example, stockbrokers are permitted to adopt a company structure rather than a partnership structure. In such cases, detailed calculations will need to be made to see whether such a step is an advantage but it needs to be borne in mind that the opportunities arising from the rules which convert accounting years to income tax years (chapter 4) will be forfeited if the activity is wholly converted to a company.

(e) There will often be substantial income tax advantages if shares in a service company are held, not by the partners themselves, but by children who have very little or no income or by the trustees of specially created settlements under which the income is accumulated. In very broad terms, if the shares are held in this way lower rates of income tax would apply on any dividends paid by the company than would otherwise be the case. Any advice that is taken about the implementation of this suggestion in particular circumstances should incorporate not only an examination of the income tax aspects but also an investigation of both the possible capital transfer tax dangers and the capital transfer tax mitigation opportunities that would flow from this type of arrangement; capital gains tax may also need to be considered.

Companies – Some Practical Reminders

Experience shows that the creation and running of a service company produce a crop of incidental problems and procedural steps. A service company structure will also create a number of incidental advantages and disadvantages, depending upon the precise individual circumstances. Here then are brief comments on some of these incidental aspects based on practical experience in this particular field:

(1) In general terms, it is not a good idea to put into a service company a business asset that will appreciate in value substantially. Suppose, for example, that a partnership creates a service company and uses it to buy an office freehold for £100,000 which then appreciates in value and is sold after a period of years for £180,000. There is a capital gain in the service company of £80,000 which will be liable to tax. But the gain (less the tax paid on it) is then locked inside the service company and if steps are taken to extract it from the company then further tax will be payable. The total tax burden on the capital gain will be greater then would have been the case had the asset been held outside the service company. Of course, in practice, non-tax matters will have to be taken into account too but, generally speaking, an appreciating asset held within a company will create a larger tax burden on any realised appreciation than would otherwise have been payable.

(2) Creaming off some of the partnership profit into a service company will obviously affect the pattern of profits in the partnership. The latter part of chapter 4 demonstrated how profit patterns can often be vital to the tax-efficiency of partnership planning. Careful attention is needed in the development of a sophisticated tax strategy to avoid a situation where the existence of a service company negates or reduces the tax benefits of a properly planned profit pattern in

the partnership.

(3) It is sometimes thought that a service company can help provide for a partner's retirement. The idea behind this is that if the partners become directors of the service company, and draw a salary from it, they can then participate in an approved pension scheme (that is, a pension scheme of the type that can be set up for directors or employees). This might give the partners a good deal more generous retirement benefits than those usually achievable by partners (these are discussed more fully in Chapter 12). But not only are the Inland Revenue taking a tough line on director-partners' remuneration (see (b) above), they have also said that they will refuse to approve pension schemes which are linked to remuneration which has been disallowed as far as the company is concerned.

(4) Where a partnership has an existing approved pension scheme for its staff, and a service company is to take over employment of the staff, the scheme will need to be modified so that the service company takes over the partnership's role in the scheme and employees' rights are preserved.

(5) It is advisable that any arrangements made between the partnership and the service company are evidenced in writing in some way. For example, there should be a document setting out the agreed terms upon which the service company will make charges to the partnership; and where office equipment, etc. is transferred from the partnership to the company a document supporting the transfer should be drawn up. The written evidence can take a variety of forms: for example, formal legal contracts, exchanges of letters, or minutes recording oral discussions.

(6) The routine consequences of transferring staff, equipment, etc. to a service company should not be overlooked. Mention has already been made at (4) above of adjustment to the pension fund but there will also be such matters as revision of employees' contracts, alterations of employers' liability insurances and other insurances and notification to land-

lords of premises that are to be occupied by the service company to be attended to.

(7) The existance of a service company is bound to cause some additional expense and inconvenience which needs to be weighed against the tax savings in appropriate cases. For example, the accounts of the service company will have to be audited and this may result in an increase in professional fees. There is also the cost of forming the company in the first place and the annual (relatively modest) fees payable to the Companies Registration Office in order to keep the company alive. And, of course, there is the inconvenience and perhaps the clerical cost of maintaining two sets of business records, one for the company and one for the partnership. Value Added Tax may also be something of an irritant because the service company will have to add this tax to the amounts that it charges the partnership. In most cases the VAT paid to the service company will effectively be set-off by the partnership so that there is no overall loss other than the cost of the book-keeping involved. But, in some cases the VAT will not be fully recoverable and will have to be taken into account as one of the costs of having a service company which will need to be measured against the tax savings.

(8) Some partnerships are anxious to give their senior employees (often referred to as associates) some stake in the activity. A service company sometimes affords the opportunity for this to be done in a way that is relatively painless to the partners since the employees can be given shares in the company rather than in the partnership.

(9) Where the partners become directors of the service company and draw remuneration, consideration needs to be given to the effect of the earnings-related national insurance scheme which came into being in April 1975; in particular, payment of directors' remuneration is likely to increase the overall national insurance burden.

(10) Special provisions exist in Section 286 Income and Corporation Taxes Act 1970 which have the effect of

charging tax where (among other things) a shareholder in a close company incurs a debt to that company and the debt is left outstanding for a period of time. The detailed rules in this section need to be taken into account in deciding the period of credit to be given by the service company to the partnership.

Would you be better off with a Company?

In conclusion, perhaps the only piece of general advice that can be given is not to accept general advice. Individual factors will usually determine whether a partnership will be better off with a company. Firms should, therefore, ensure that the advantages and disadvantages relating to their own particular circumstances are calculated and weighed in the balance in making a decision whether or not to have a company. Ideally, these calculations should be re-worked from time to time as circumstances change and fresh decisions made, if necessary.

CHAPTER TWELVE

SOME SPECIAL PARTNERSHIP SITUATIONS

This final chapter deals with mergers, losses and retirement. Some aspects of these topics are highly complex and technical and some can only be adequately discussed against the background of the special financial circumstances of a particular partnership and its partners. Because of this, the topics are dealt with in technical outline only and are not given the extensive treatment afforded to other subjects in this book.

MERGERS – ARE THE OPENING YEARS AND CLOSING YEARS RULES BROUGHT INTO PLAY?

Chapter 4 included an explanation of the special rules applicable in the early years of a new partnership and the closing years of a partnership. Difficult problems are often encountered in practice about the application of these rules when partnership businesses merge. In the discussion that follows, the merger of two partnerships into one will be considered (the case of Firm A and Firm B merging into Firm AB); the discussion may be adapted to meet the case of a greater number of partnerships merging into one.

There are many different approaches to the problem and the correct approach will depend to a great extent upon the precise facts of individual cases. It is convenient to consider the differing approaches under four heads and, in comparing the advantages and disadvantages of each method, the reader should bear in mind that treating a partnership business as having closed will bring about the tax benefit of the pass-over period (to use the terminology adopted in chapter 4) while, on the other side of the coin, treating a new business as having commenced will bring about the tax disadvantage of the multiplication of profits (also described in chapter 4).

1. The facts may show that both Firm A and Firm B have closed their old business activities and that Firm AB has factually started a new one. This may be the case even though all of the old partners are continuing in the new Firm AB from the same addresses as before. For example, in the 1934 case of George Humphries & Co v Cook, Mr. Humphries was in business as a film processor. The technical work involved in this business was sub-contracted to a Mr. Terraneau. On 1 April 1930, Humphries took Terraneau into partnership and the film processing activity was continued as previously for the same customers. The Inland Revenue argued that on 1 April 1930 a totally new business came into existence and the Court upheld this argument.

The Humphries case is possibly an extreme example but it may be relevant in an argument that because the combined clients or customers of Firm AB are a different group from the separate clients or customers of Firm A and Firm B then the two old partnerships have in a factual sense ceased and a new one has commenced. If this is so, then the closing year rules will be applied to each of Firm A and Firm B and the early years rules will be applied to Firm AB. Whether this is beneficial or not will depend upon whether the profits of the pass-over period are greater or less than the profits of the period of multiplication of profits. Where this factual closure and factual commencement situation arises, the options which apply when there is a change in partners (described in chapter 5) will have no application.

2. If the facts are such that Firm AB is no different from the previous Firm A and Firm B it could be said that both of the old partnerships are continuing in merged form. In most instances, the Inland Revenue

are prepared to accept that this has happened. The partnership change rules (chapter 5) now come into operation. The result is that the firms have the choice of either treating Firm A and Firm B as having closed and Firm AB as having commenced (that is, with the same practical effect as in 1 above) or alternatively to continue the income tax assessments on a preceding-year basis. If the latter method is chosen the Inland Revenue will assess the first few years of Firm AB by looking at the combined profits in the preceding-year of both Firm A and Firm B together.

3. A more complex variation (but one with potentially greater tax benefits) is where Firm A factually ceases operation and the partners of Firm A are then taken into Firm B as partners in that firm. If this happens then Firm A will enjoy a pass-over period because it has closed. Turning to Firm B, this partnership has had a change in its partners and it therefore has the choice of action described in chapter 5. It may either treat itself as having closed and re-opened or the assessments may continue on the preceding-year basis. The preceding year profits will be the profits of Firm B only. The effect of all this is that Firm A has enjoyed a pass-over period without there necessarily being a period of multiplication of profits to counteract the benefits. This may produce very substantial tax savings. The Inland Revenue may attempt a counter-argument, depending on whether the facts support this, that after the "merger" Firm B developed a new business activity (namely, the activity previously carried on by Firm A) and that the additional profits generated in Firm B by that new activity have to be charged to tax by applying the early rules. If, on the facts of a particular case, this Inland Revenue argument were to succeed, then there would be the tax disadvantage of a multiplication of profits.
4. This approach is the converse of 3 above: the business of Firm B factually closes down and the partners of Firm B are taken in as partners in Firm A. The consequences are broadly as in 3 above but the pass-over period will now appear in Firm B rather than in Firm

A. In broad terms, if the pre-"merger" profits of Firm B are running at a higher level than those of Firm A, there is a greater tax advantage in having the pass-over period in Firm B rather than in Firm A.

Of course, where more than two firms are involved the possibilities (and the complications; and the opportunities for tax saving) increase.

Differing sets of facts obviously produce differing results and, in some respects at least, the facts will depend upon the way in which the merger is organised. Where the amounts involved are substantial, it is therefore advisable to take top-level tax advice *before* the precise form of the merger is agreed and *before* any announcements are made to clients, customers and other third parties regarding the merger.

LOSSES

Sometimes a partnership will make a loss for tax purposes. This does not necessarily indicate that the partnership is on the road to ruin; the stock relief and capital allowance rules mean that a partnership, especially a manufacturing or dealing firm, may well have a loss for tax purposes while it has a profit in its accounts.

A partnership of course has a loss when its computation of "profits" for tax purposes for an accounting year, after deduction of stock relief and capital allowances, throws up a minus figure. (We do not deal here with capital losses, as for example where a partnership sells an investment for less than it paid for it — this unfortunately is outside the scope of this book.) What happens then?

Let us make it clear that how the partnership actually copes with the loss in real life is irrelevant. They may meet it out of capital, or inject further capital into the business, or borrow; these things may have tax consequences of their own, but they do not affect how the accrued loss is dealt with for tax.

What happens is that there are some reasonably generous rules whereby the partners can set that loss against other income of theirs, thus reducing their tax bills. Each partner is treated separately, that is you work out a partner's share of the loss, just like you work out his share of profits, and each partner chooses separately what to do with his share.

First, and simplest, he can carry his share of the loss forward indefinitely and set it against his share of future profits of the business. But this is not ideal because he has to wait before it results in any reduction in his tax bill, and if the worst comes to the worst the business may never make any profit in the future.

The second method of dealing with a loss has technical complexities. In most cases it has the following effect: the partner can set his share of the loss against *any* income of his for the tax year in question or the preceding tax year.

Example 12.1
Nadir & Partners make a loss for the year ending 31 December 1978. Mr. Smith is a partner and his share of the loss is £8,000. Had there been a profit for the year his share would have counted as his income for 1979/80. Mr Smith can set £8,000 loss against any income of his for 1979/80 or 1978/79.

For 1978/79 Mr. Smith had a share of profit from the firm – £5,000 – derived from the accounting year ending 31 December 1977, and investment income of another £5,000. He chooses to offset his loss against his 1978/79 income. He has to set the £8,000 against the profits first, so £5,000 is set against them, reducing them to nil, and £3,000 against the investment income, reducing it to £2,000. (Ideally one would be able to offset losses against investment income first, thus minimising the investment income surcharge, but the rules say you have to set it against earnings first.)

In this way Mr. Smith gets relief for his loss at once in the form of tax refunds for 1978/79. (Had his income for 1978/79 not been enough to mop up his loss he could have set the balance of the loss against his income for 1979/80, and any remaining balance he could have carried forward against future profits of the business in accordance with the first method of dealing with losses.)

New businesses and new partners

A person who starts a new business has a special privilege. If he makes a loss in any of his first three years he can carry the loss back and set it against any income of his of the three years prior to the year of the loss. This rule also applies to a new partner in an established partnership.

The second method of dealing with losses, and the special privilege for new businesses, only apply if the business in question is being carried on on a commercial basis and with a view to making a profit. In other words if partners run a business more or less as a hobby, the legislation provides, not altogether unreasonably, that they cannot make use of its losses except by carrying them forward against future profits of the business, if any.

PROVIDING INCOME DURING RETIREMENT

There are a variety of practical approaches to the problem of creating income during a partner's period of retirement and the most tax-efficient methods are usually those which utilise insurance schemes of one sort or another. The principal practical methods of providing retirement income are noted below; the working details of the insurance-backed arrangements are not discussed in depth since readers will generally obtain details of the schemes applicable to themselves from their insurance brokers and financial counsellors. In some cases, it may be necessary to consider a mixture of the approaches described below rather than to select just one.

Retirement Annuity

This is virtually a do-it-yourself pension scheme which enables a partner to make contributions to a fund (which has to be approved by the Inland Revenue) in order to create a pension for himself at some future time. A variety of names are used for these schemes including self-employed person's retirement annuities and self-employed deferred annuities.

The amounts contributed to the scheme by the partner are (within stated limits) fully allowable for tax against his earned income so that he obtains tax relief by effectively lopping off his top slice of earned income at the rate applicable to that top slice. He is entitled to take part of his pension as a commuted lump sum and if he does so the lump sum is tax-free. He is also entitled to use the scheme to provide a pension to his widow or dependants or a lump sum payable on his death. Apart from these options, he cannot use the amount he has invested in a retirement annuity scheme for purposes other than providing himself with a pension; he cannot, for example, "cash in" the scheme after a period of years and extract a lump sum. And when the partner receives his pension under his retirement annuity scheme this will be taxed as earned income and not investment income (assuming, as will usually be the case, that his contributions to the scheme did not exceed the laid-down limits).

The amount which can be paid into a retirement annuity scheme and for which tax relief is claimable is limited to a percentage of the partner's share of profits for the income tax year in question. The percentage is currently 15% with an increase for partners who were born in 1915 or earlier. For these older partners the percentage is somewhat higher (depending upon age) reaching a maximum of 30% for those born in 1907 or earlier. There is another limit on the tax-allowable contributions that may be made to a retirement annuity scheme: the maximum for any one tax year is £3,000 and this of course has the effect of cutting off the 15% allowable amount when earnings reach £20,000. As is to be expected, the maximum is somewhat higher for partners born in 1915 or earlier, reaching £6,000 for those born in 1907 or earlier. (The amounts of £3,000 and £6,000 apply to income tax years from 6 April 1977 onwards. The limits were lower previously.)

The percentage limits are percentages of the partner's share of profits for tax purposes after deduction of capital allowances *but before deduction of stock relief and overseas work relief.*

The basic rule is that the various limits are calculated from the partner's share of profits for the income tax year *in which* the contribution is paid. But there is a useful feature which enables a partner to calculate and pay a maximum contribution into a retirement annuity scheme in a case where his share of partnership profits is calculated only after the end of the income tax year. The rule is that if a partner pays a retirement annuity contribution within six months after any particular income tax assessment has become final and conclusive then he may claim to throw back the payment and claim relief for it against the tax assessment concerned. If, for example, there has been delay in agreeing a partnership's income tax assessment for 1978/79 and it is finally agreed with the Inspector of Taxes on 1 June 1979 then the partners may pay contributions into a retirement annuity scheme at any time until the end of November 1979 and make a claim (before the six months expire) to obtain tax relief for the payment in the 1978/79 tax calculations.

Company Pension Scheme

Many partnerships will have set up pension schemes for their employees but, unfortunately, partners cannot join such schemes as they are not employed, using the word in its technical sense. But if the partnership is run in tandem with a company there is conceivably scope for the partners' joining a pension scheme run by the company. This was discussed in Chapter 11.

Combined Endowment Insurance and Annuity

Under this approach, the partner takes out a conventional endowment policy on his life to mature on the date of his retirement. The proceeds are then invested in the purchase of an annuity. The annuity, when it is received, is only partly taxable; only what is usually called the interest element in the annuity is taxed, the remainder escaping tax completely since it is no more than a repayment of the purchase price of the annuity.

An advantage of this approach is that an endowment policy, unlike contributions to a retirement annuity scheme, can, if necessary, be turned into hard cash.

But a major disadvantage is that the contributions by the partner enjoy only modest tax relief: 17½% of the contributions are an allowable deduction for tax purposes.

Annuity from the Partnership

Some partnership agreements provide that when a partner retires he, and perhaps his widow and dependants, will receive a periodical payment (an annuity) from the remaining partners. The practical effect of the tax statutes is to give an income tax allowance to the payers of the annuity at whatever is their appropriate rates of income tax and to tax the annuity in the hands of the recipient as if it were earned income.

There is a limit though beyond which the annuity will not be treated as earned income in the recipient's hands. In broad terms, it is necessary to look at the last seven income tax years in which the retired partner was a full-time working partner and to take the best three of those years. The retired partner's share of the income tax assessment for these three best years is taken and is averaged to produce a one-year figure. If the annuity is not more than 50% of this one-year figure it will be treated entirely as earned income but if it exceeds the 50% limit the excess will be taxed as investment income.

A procedural point: when the annuity is paid, income tax at the basic rate will be deducted by the payers and effectively accounted for the Inland Revenue. The recipient will receive the annuity already taxed at the basic rate and, where appropriate, the tax will be adjusted up or down by the Inland Revenue.

Consultancy Fees

After a partner has retired, he may receive fees from the partnership for consultancy services either as a free-lance consultant or as an employee of the firm. The fees will be taxed as earned income in his hands and will be allowed as an expense to the partnership. But if the fees are excessive in relation to the services rendered by the ex-partner then the Inland Revenue will be able to refuse a full allowance for them in calculating the firm's profits. This may prove a stumbling block where, for example, a partner has retired overseas and has virtually no contact with this country. In these circumstances, an annuity from the partnership may need to be considered rather than a consultancy fee, since it is not necessary to demonstrate that an annuity is justified by services rendered. In regard to the specific situation of an ex-partner who has retired overseas, an annuity may present other advantages since there is the possibility that the double taxation agreement between the United Kingdom and the country to which the partner has retired may provide some tax exemption on annuity income.

A drawback of the consultancy fee arrangement is that it does not normally lend itself to making provision for a widow or dependants.

Continuing as a Part-time Partner

In some respects, this approach is a development of the consultancy fees arrangement. Instead of a partner completely retiring he may reduce the level of his activity to a relatively insignificant amount. He would have to continue to be a genuine partner though because so long as he was active to some extent as a partner his remuneration or profit-share would be treated as earned income in his hands and would effectively reduce the income tax payable by the other partners. The drawbacks are that his widow and dependants would not be provided for and he would remain liable for the partnership's debts while he was a part-time partner.

EPILOGUE

We hope that readers are now feeling more cheerful about partnership taxation. Once the basic principles are grasped it suddenly becomes a much less frightening subject. We have tried not only to explain the rules but also to point out where possible straightforward ideas for minimising tax liability.

Reading this book does not mean that readers will never need to take professional advice - far from it: and some will want to seek out top-level advice with a view to putting through a major tax saving exercise. But we hope that readers are now more confident about deciding when they do need outside advice and when they do not, and feel equipped to talk to the Inland Revenue and their accountants on something more like equal terms.

TECHNICAL SUPPLEMENT
(including Statutory and Case references)

These notes and references are provided to enable readers and their advisers to investigate particular problems in greater depth. The abbreviations used are as follows:

AC	Appeal Cases
All ER	All England Law Reports
CAA 1968	Capital Allowances Act 1968
CGTA 1979	Capital Gains Tax Act 1979
FA (1975 etc)	Finance Act (1975 etc)
F(2)A 1975	Finance (No. 2) Act 1975
KB	King's Bench Division Reports
QBD	Queen's Bench Division Reports
S	Section
SC	Court of Session Cases
Sch	Schedule
STC	Simons Tax Cases
STI	Simons Tax Intelligence
TA 1970	Income and Corporation Taxes Act 1970
TC	Tax Cases (published by the Inland Revenue)
TMA 1970	Taxes Management Act 1970

Page		
	Chapter 1	
4	Joint income tax assessment	S152 TA 1970 There is useful discussion, especially about the effect of the death of a partner, in Harrison v Willis Bros (1965) 43 TC 61; (1965) 3 All ER 753
4	Partnership law and debts	S9 Partnership Act 1890
5	Individual liability to capital gains tax	S60 CGTA 1979
	Chapter 2	
8	"... the full amount of the profits or gains ..."	S115 TA 1970
8	The fundamental rule	See, for example, Gresham Life Assurance Society v Styles (1892)3 TC 185; (1892) AC 309. Also Sun Insurance v Clark (1912)6 TC 49; (1912) AC 443

Page		
8	Case History 2.1	Walker v Carnaby Harrower, Barham & Pykett (1969) 46 TC 561; (1970) 1 A11 ER 502. The principle of not taxing certain gratuitous receipts has been applied again more recently in Simpson v John Reynolds & Co (Insurances) Ltd (1975) STC 271; (1975) 2 A11 ER 88, and in Murray v Goodhews (1978) STC 207; (1978)2 A11 ER 40. For a case which went the other way, because the payment was solicited and was a reward for work done, see McGowan v Brown and Cousins (1977) STC 342; (1977)3 A11 ER 844.
	Chapter 3	
14	Capital gains: special rules about expenses	S32 CGTA 1979
15	Ordinary accounting principles	See the notes regarding "the fundamental rule" at chapter 2 above
15	Lothian Chemical Co.Ltd v Rogers	(1926) 11 TC 508
16	Heather v PE Consulting Group Ltd	(1972)48 TC 193; (1973)1 A11 ER 8
16	"Wholly and exclusively"	S130(a) TA 1970. This wording can be traced back as far as S100 of the Income Tax Act 1842!
17	Case history 3.1	Bowden v Russell & Russell (1965) 42 TC 301; (1965)2 All ER 258
19	Copeman v William Flood & Sons Ltd	(1941)24 TC 53; (1941)1KB 202
20	Caillebotte v Quinn	(1975)STC265; (1975)2 All ER 412
21	Non-allowance of capital expenditure	This principle can be derived from "the fundamental rule" (see chapter 2) or from S130(f) TA 1970
22	Accountancy treatment as a factor	The case of ECC Quarries Ltd v Watkis (1975) STC 578; (1975)3 All ER 843 contains a review of the significance of accountancy treatment in deciding whether expenditure is capital or revenue. The case also confirms that ultimately the question is one of law.
22	Atherton v British Insulated and Helsby Cables Ltd	(1926)10 TC 155; (1926) AC 205
23	Associated Portland Cement Manufacturers Ltd v Kerr	(1945)27 TC 103; (1946)1 All ER 68
23	Pitt v Castle Mill Warehousing Co. Ltd	(1974) STC 420; (1974)3 All ER 146. The three-part test put forward in this case was repeated in a

Page		
		decision in June 1975: ECC Quarries Ltd v Watkis (1975) STC 578; (1975)3 All ER 843
25	Inland Revenue v Law Shipping Co. Ltd	(1923)12 TC 621; (1924)SC 74
26	Odeon Associated Theatres Ltd v Jones	(1971)48 TC 279; (1972)1 All ER 681
28	Covenant in lease to carry out initial repairs	This was specifically considered in Jackson v Laskers Home Furnishers Ltd (1956)37 TC 69; (1956)3 All ER 891. The Laskers decision was approved by Buckley LJ in Odeon Associated Theatres Ltd v Jones. The tenant is not likely to get any relief under the premium provisions: proviso to S 80(2) TA 1970
29	Entertaining and gifts	S411 TA 1970
29	Overseas customers and entertaining	S 411(2) & S 411(6) TA 1970
30	Staff entertaining	S 411(5) TA 1970
30	Business gifts	S 411(8) TA 1970 as amended
30	Lease premiums and other lease payments	S 134 TA 1970 read with S 80 TA 1970. Note also the definitions in S 90 TA 1970
32	Case history 3.3	This is an adaptation of Banning v Wright (1972)48 TC 421; (1972)2 All ER 987
33	Payment for varying or waiving a provision of lease	S 80(4) TA 1970 read with S 134 TA 1970
33	Acquiring tail-end of lease	S 134(2) TA 1970
34	Redundancy payments	S 412 TA 1970. Payments for unfair dismissal under the Employment Protection Act 1975 are not specifically allowed, but where the business is continuing are allowable on general principles.
35	Southern v Borax Consolidated Ltd	(1940)23 TC 597; (1940)4 All ER 412
35	Salaries etc. paid to partners	They could be disallowed alternatively under S 130(b) TA 1970
35	Salaried partners	A case on this is Stekel v Ellice (1973)1 All ER 465, where the judge said that every case must be considered on its own facts
36	Tax on investment income	S 32(1) FA 1971
36	Loans and lettings on favourable terms	A loan repayable on demand or a week-to-week or month-to-month letting will not attract capital transfer tax: S 115(1) and (7) FA 1976. A loan or letting ex-

Page		
		pressed to be for a longer period will attract tax not under S 115 (S 115(3)) but on the general principles of CTT. For capital gains tax on lettings see S19(3) and Sch 3 CGTA 1979.
	Chapter 4	
	Chapter 4 generally	The chapter deals with the normal case of a business preparing accounts for regular 12-monthly periods. The consequences of preparing accounts for a period of other than 12 months are considerable; they can be advantageous or disadvantageous depending on the precise individual circumstances. The Board of Inland Revenue have issued an extremely useful (but technical) leaflet explaining the consequences in detail with worked examples. The leaflet is entitled "Income Tax Assessments on Business Profits – Changes of Accounting Date" and is available from the Board of Inland Revenue, Somerset House, Strand, London WC2R 1LB. The leaflet should be very carefully studied before a decision is taken to change an accounting date. There is also a useful reported case on the subject: Inland Revenue v Helical Bar Ltd 1972 48 TC 221; 1 All ER 1205.
39	Period of assessment for companies	S 247 TA 1970
40	Assessment of rent received	S 67 TA 1970 – see paragraph 2 of Schedule A – and S 69 TA 1970
40	Assessment of interest received	Principally S 119 to S 124 TA 1970
40	Assessment of capital gains	S4(1) CGTA 1979
41	Method of granting capital allowances	S70(2) and S 72 CAA 1968
46	Preceding-year basis	S 115(2)(a) TA 1970
46	Income tax year 1	S 116(1) TA 1970
47	Income tax year 2	S 116(2) TA 1970
49	What if profits fall away?	S 117(1) and (2) TA 1970
50	Partnership change	S 154 TA 1970
50	No tax assessments after business closes	The fundamental principle of tax law referred to is derived from National Provident Institution v Brown (1921)8 TC 57; (1921)2 AC 222. Although this case concerned the taxability of discounts earned on Treasury Bills, one of the gen-

Page		
		eral points it decided was that in order to be taxable for a particular year on income from a particular source, the source had to be held in the year.
52	Closing tax year	S 118(1)(a) TA 1970
52	CTY – 1 and CTY – 2	S 118(1)(b) TA 1970
61	Separate partnerships	An old but useful case on the existence of separate partnerships is Farrell v Sunderland Steamship Co. Ltd (1903)4 TC 605
62	What of the Future?	The Public Accounts Committee, which is a committee of backbench MPs, has recommended switching to an actual profits basis if possible and that consideration should be given to enacting in the meanwhile measures to prevent exploitation of the cessation and recommencement rules. (Sixth Report from the Committee of Public Accounts, Session 1977/78, HMSO). The Inland Revenue have said that they are examining the whole question but an actual profits basis of assessment has problems of its own and they have not yet reached any conclusion on the matter (Inland Revenue Press Release 9 October 1978: (1978) STI 480).
	Chapter 5	
	Chapter 5 generally	The income tax code on changes in partnerships is contained in S 154 TA 1970 as amended. The technical reader is reminded that, quite apart from the income tax consequences dealt with in the chapter, a change in the partners may produce capital gains tax consequences, particularly where money changes hands or partnership assets are revalued. The problem is aired in a statement issued by the Inland Revenue in January 1975 entitled "Capital gains tax: partnerships" available from the Board of Inland Revenue, Somerset House, Strand, London WC2R 1LB; it is also printed at (1975) STI 17. In certain respects, the practices suggested in this statement do not accord with the strict law, especially what is now S 19(3) CGTA 1979.

Page	**Chapter 6**	
74	Headings of capital expenditure	See, for example, CAA 1968 and Part XIV TA 1970
75	Yarmouth v France	(1887) 19 QBD 647
75	What constitutes machinery or plant	An informative document is a press release by the Consultative Committee of Accountancy Bodes dated 9 August 1977. This contains the Revenue's views on whether various items do or do not constitute machinery and plant in the case of new hotels, but in our opinion these views can be treated as applying to any business. Copies of the press release are obtainable from the Consultative Committee of Accountancy Bodies, Publications Department, P.O. Box 433, Chartered Accountants' Hall, Moorgate Place, London EC2P 2BJ, enclosing a stamped addressed envelope.
76	First-year allowances	S 41 and S 42 FA 1971 as amended
77	Part-claim or no claim of first-year allowances	S 41(3) FA 1971
77	Ships	Para 8 Sch 8 FA 1971
78	"Related accounts year" – basis period	S 72 CAA 1968 and S 50(2) FA 1971
79	Qualifying for first-year allowances	S 41(1) and S 50(4) FA 1971
80	Significance of 5 April re equipment purchases	The date 5 April is also relevant during the early and closing years of a business: see S 72(2) CAA 1968 as applied by S 50(2) FA 1971
80	Hire purchase	S 45 FA 1971
81	Regional development grants	S 84(1) CAA 1968 as amended and para 15 Sch 8 FA 1971
81	Motor vehicles	S 43 FA 1971 and para 9 to para 11 Sch 8 FA 1971 as amended
83	Private use of cars	Para 5 Sch 8 FA 1971
84	Pool of expenditure	S 44 FA 1971
84	Pre-October 1970 expenditure	S 39 FA 1976
87	Different treatment of car and generator	S 44(4)(a)(ii) FA 1971
87	Sales of equipment and cars	S 44 FA 1971. Note that in the relatively rare case of the sale proceeds exceeding the cost, only the cost is deducted from the pool: proviso to S 44(6) FA 1971
88	Separate pool for quality car	Para 10 Sch 8 FA 1971 as amended
90	Claiming and "disclaiming" first-year allowances	S 70(3) CAA 1968 and S 48(4) FA 1971; S 41(3) FA 1971. The true position is unclear. The Inland Revenue say that they are prepared to consider allowing a first-

Page		
		year allowance claim to be withdrawn where a partner's circumstances change between the date of the assessment's becoming final and the end of the tax year in question: (1978) STI 321
90	Part-claim or no claim of writing-down allowance	Proviso to S 44(2) FA 1971
91	Renewals basis	There seems to be no precise statutory authority for this long-established basis but there is some statutory support for it in S 130(d) TA 1970
92	Leasing quality cars	The restriction is in para 12 Sch 8 FA 1971. But by para 9 the restriction does not apply to cars which fall within S 43(c) FA 1971. S 43 (c) specifies cars which are provided "wholly or mainly for hire to .... members of the public in the ordinary course of a trade".
94	Partnership change treated as a continuation	The effect of S 154 (2) TA 1970 is to leave the capital allowances undisturbed. Note also, with regard to machinery and plant, S 48(3) and S 48(4) CAA 1968 as amended by para 15(3) Sch 8 FA 1971; and with regard to other expenditure, note S 79(2) CAA 1968
94	Partnership change treated as a discontinuance	The statutory provisions touching upon this subject are: S48 CAA 1968 as amended by para 15(3) Sch 8 FA 1971; S 79 CAA 1968 (for expenditure other than machinery and plant); para 4 Sch 7 CAA 1968; para 3(1) Sch 8 FA 1971 read with S 44(6) FA 1971; para 13 Sch 8 FA 1971
94	Assets belonging to individual partner	S 44 CAA 1968 and para 15(1) Sch 8 FA 1971
	Chapter 7	
98	Industrial buildings defined	S 7 CAA 1968 and (hotels) S 39 FA 1978
99	Kilmarnock Equitable Co-op Society v Inland Revenue	(1966)42 TC 675
100	Bourne v Norwich Crematorium	(1967)44 TC 164; (1967)2 All ER 576
100	Sports pavilions	S 10 CAA 1968
100	Buildings partly industrial	S 7(4) CAA 1968
100	Initial allowance	S1 CAA 1968 as amended. For hotels the rate is only 20%: para 1 Sch 6 FA 1978
101	Annual writing-down allowance	S 2 CAA 1968
101	Buying a used building	S 2(3) and S 2(4) CAA 1968

Page		
103	Jarrold v John Good & Sons Ltd	(1962)40 TC 681; (1963) 1 All ER 141
	Chapter 8	
106	Rules of stock relief	Sch 5 FA 1976. The legislation says (para 30) that *completed* work does not count as work-in-progress (there is no equivalent rule for trade stock) but the Inland Revenue have announced that they will apply relief to completed work except in exceptional circumstances: (1977) STI 34. *Billed* work however does not count as work-in-progress.
108	Payments on account of work-in-progress	Para 29(4) Sch 5 FA 1976
108	Opening or closing of business or change of accounts date	Paras 2(2), 4, 22 and 23 Sch 5 FA 1976
108	Stock relief for accounting years ending before 6 April 1975	Sch 10 F(2)A 1975, and see also paras 13 to 18 Sch 5 FA 1976
109	Claw-back	Para 2(1) Sch 5 FA 1976
110	Partnership changes	Para 21 read with para 2(2) Sch 5 FA 1976
111	Time limit for claim	Para 1(3) Sch 5 FA 1976
	Chapter 9	
113	Relief for employees working abroad	S 31 & Sch 7 FA 1977
113	Relief for partners working abroad	S 27 & Sch 4 FA 1978
114	30-day rule	S 27(1)(c) FA 1978
114	Employee's uplift claim	Para 4 Sch 7 FA 1977
115	Employee who spends 365 days abroad	Para 1 Sch 7 FA 1977
115	Partner must claim relief	S 27(5) FA 1978
115	Day of work abroad	S 27(2) FA 1978
117	Overseas partnership	S 153 & S 122(1) TA 1970 and S 23 FA 1974. A partner who is resident in the UK but is either (i) domiciled abroad or (ii) a British subject or citizen of the Irish Republic ordinarily resident abroad, is taxable on profits from such a partnership on the remittance basis instead of being entitled to the 25% reduction: S 122 TA 1970 as amended
117	No double relief	S 27(4) FA 1978
117	Overseas partnership: technical assessment rules	The rules for calculating the tax liability of an overseas partnership (Case V of Schedule D) (S 122 to S 124 TA 1970 as amended

Page		
		and S 23 FA 1974) are different in certain respects from the rules of Cases I and II. For example a change in the composition of the partnership is not a cessation of the business: S23(6)(b) FA 1974
	Chapter 10	
120	Interest on house purchase loan	S 75 and Part I Sch 9 FA 1972 as amended and S 19 and Part II Sch I FA 1974 as amended. It is assumed that Stan does not have any investment income; if he did the mortgage interest would be set against that first, thus minimising the investment income surcharge
120	Students	S 26 FA 1977
120	Children resident overseas	S 25 FA 1977 and S 20(5) FA 1978
121	Income tax rates for 1978/79	S 13 FA 1978
122	Basic and other rates of tax	S 32 FA 1971 as amended
123	Date of payment of tax	S 4 TA 1970 as amended
123	Date of payment of tax – effect of delay in agreeing tax	S 55 TMA 1970 as substituted
	Chapter 11	
128	Companies do not pay income tax	S 238(2) TA 1970; but a non-resident company is liable to income tax on UK income.
129	Basic rate tax deemed to have been paid on dividends	S 86 FA 1972
132	Reduced rate of corporation tax	S 95 FA 1972 as amended
133	No preceding year basis	S 247 TA 1970; S 243(3) TA 1970
134	Date of payment of corporation tax	S 243(4) & S 244 TA 1970; S 84 & S 85 FA 1972
136	Close companies – definition	S 282, S 283, S 302 and S 303 TA 1970 as amended
136	Shortfall rules	Sch 16 FA 1972 as amended
137	Shortfall escape route	Para 8 Sch 16 FA 1972 as amended
137	Abatement relief	Para 9 Sch 16 FA 1972 as amended The new threshold figures (see below) apply to accounting periods ending after 26 October 1977.

The rule (in a case where there are no associated companies) is that where a company's after-tax profits are £25,000 or less there can be no shortfall liability. Where a company's after-tax profits are between £25,000 and £75,000 the company's after-tax profits are reduced for the purposes of calculating shortfall liability by the following amount.

$$\frac{£75{,}000 - £A}{2}$$

where £A is the after-tax profit. The figure of £45,402 is arrived at as follows:

Page

Net profits (assuming they are wholly estate or trading income)	£45,402
Less corporation tax @ 42%	19,069
After-tax profits	26,333
Less abatement $\frac{£75{,}000 - £26{,}333}{2}$	24,333
	2,000
Profits prima facie apportionable (50% of £2,000)	1,000

The £1,000 is not in fact apportionable because of a separate rule, brought in mainly for administrative convenience, that a sum of £1,000 or less is not apportionable: para 1(3) Sch 16 FA 1972.

The figure of £156,250 is arrived at as follows:

Net profits (assuming they are wholly estate or trading income)	156,250
Less corporation tax @ 52%	81,250
After-tax profits	75,000

This is the lowest level of profit at which there is no abatement relief.

Page		
141	Case history	Stephenson v Payne, Stone, Fraser & Co. (1968)44 TC 507; (1968) 1 All ER 524
148	Approved pension scheme	Chapter II Part II FA 1970. Note that the Inland Revenue has no choice but to approve certain schemes: S 19 FA 1970
	Chapter 12	
152	Geo. Humphries & Co v Cook	(1934) 19 TC 121
155	First method of dealing with losses	S 171 TA 1970
155	Second method of dealing with losses	S 168 TA 1970. Technical readers will recognise that the treatment in the text is very simplified
156	New businesses	S 30 FA 1978
156	On a commercial basis and with a view to making profit	S 170 TA 1970; and S 30(4) FA 1978 (where the wording is stricter). There are further restrictions for farming and market gardening businesses: S 180 TA 1970
156	Retirement annuity	S 226 – S 228 TA 1970 as amended
158	Retirement annuity – six months rule	S 227 (3) TA 1970 as substituted. For the Inland Revenue's views on when an assessment is final and conclusive, see Taxation Magazine (1977) Vol 100 p 45
158	Purchased annuity only partly taxable	S 230 TA 1970

Page		
158	Endowment insurance – tax relief	S 19 TA 1970 as amended and para 5 Sch 4 FA 1976
158	Annuity from the partnership	To ensure that the annuity provides tax relief to the payers at the higher rates of tax, consideration needs to be given to S 457 TA 1970 as amended
159	Annuity from the partnership – earned income in recipient's hands	S 16 FA 1974
159	Deduction of tax from annuity	S 52 & S 53 TA 1970 as amended
159	Excessive consultancy fees	S 130(a) TA 1970
160	Part-time partner – earned income	S 530(1)(c) TA 1970
160	Part-time partner – liability for debts	S 9 Partnership Act 1890

INDEX

PARTNERSHIP TAXATION

– a practical guide

UP-DATING SUPPLEMENT, JANUARY 1981

The book incorporates tax changes up to and including the 1978 Finance Act. This updating supplement is concerned with changes in law and practice since that time: in particular the changes made in the 1979 and 1980 Finance Acts, and the stock relief changes proposed in November 1980.

Rates of Tax

The general level of income tax was significantly reduced with effect from 6th April 1979. The top rate of income tax on earned income is now 60% (compared with 83% previously) and the maximum rate of income tax on investment income is now 75%. The 25% "lower rate" of income tax has been abolished.

The rates of tax for the year ending 5th April 1981 are shown below.

p. 120

Band of Income	Rate
First £11,250	30%
£11,251 to £13,250	40%
£13,251 to £16,750	45%
£16,751 to £22,250	50%
£22,251 to £27,750	55%
Over £27,750	60%

The additional tax on investment income remains at 15% and is generally applicable where investment income exceeds £5,500 (Section 18 Finance Act 1980).

p. 21 **Pre-business and Post-business expenses**

Relief is now available for expenses incurred before the commencement of business provided that they are incurred not more than one year before the commencement of business and would have qualified for relief if they had been incurred after commencement. (Section 39 Finance Act 1980)

p. 34 **Redundancy Payments**

Under general tax law, severance payments made to employees on the termination of a business would not usually be allowable as a tax deduction since they would not be made for the purpose of earning profits. There has for a number of years, however, been a specific provision allowing a tax deduction for statutory redundancy payments. A new provision has been introduced to allow relief for certain "golden handshakes" made in conjunction with redundancy payments on the closure of a business provided that the golden handshake does not exceed three times the redundancy payment. (Section 41 Finance Act 1980).

p. 62 **Income Tax Basis Years – What of the Future?**

The Inland Revenue have been making a detailed study of the present and alternative bases of assessment for income tax purposes. The Inland Revenue say that the studies are more or less complete but they have not yet been considered by the Board of Inland Revenue, being the senior officials who will decide upon any recommendation to the Government for legislative change. In response to a recent Parliamentary question in the House of Commons on whether the Government have any plans to change the rules, Mr. Rees, a Government Minister, replied:

"We have at present no such plans".

It therefore appears that the Government are waiting for the Inland Revenue to report to them on the subject but it is considered unlikely that a change in rules will be made. If a change in the rules were proposed, a considerable period of public consultation and debate would be required before acceptable practical proposals could be agreed upon, including suitable transitional provisions.

pp. 81-88 **Equipment, Machinery and Plant**

The method of calculating capital allowances has been altered by the Finance Act 1980 in relation to expenditure on non-quality cars. The new rules require future expenditure on non-quality cars and their proceeds on sale to be dealt with as a separate pool of expenditure. The generous treatment referred to on page 88 where the equipment is sold will therefore no longer generally be available. (Section 69 Finance Act 1980).

It will still be necessary to separate quality cars into a special separate pool for *each car*. The Finance (No. 2) Act 1979 increased the cost limits here from £5,000 to £8,000 in the case of cars bought after 12th June 1979. The maximum annual writing down allowance for quality cars is, as a result, now £2,000 (Section 14 Finance (No 2) Act 1979).

Leasing quality cars – the established loophole referred to on page 93 no longer exists as a result of changes made in the Finance (No. 2) Act 1979. Now, where a lease of a quality car is taken out after 12th June 1979, a restriction applies so that only a percentage of the hire charge is an allowable expense. This affects the Lease or Buy table on page 93 – full rentals will no longer be allowed in either the short or long run where a passenger car costing more than £8,000 (when new) is leased. The proportion of the leasing charge allowable is computed as follows:-

$$\frac{\text{£8,000}}{\text{£8,000} + \tfrac{1}{2}\text{ excess of cost over £8,000}} \times \text{leasing charge}$$

The loophole resulted from an imprecise definition of private motor car in relation to leased cars. The new legislation altered the former definition (Section 14 Finance (No. 2) Act 1979).

p. 101 **Allowances on Buildings**

A special improved initial allowance of 100% has been introduced for small industrial buildings. A small industrial building is one which has a gross internal floor space less than 2,500 sq. ft. However, no change has been made to the definition of industrial buildings, which remains somewhat restrictive. (Section 75 Finance Act 1980).

Special new reliefs were introduced in the Finance Act 1980 for expenditure on industrial and commercial buildings in certain areas to be designated "Enterprise Zones". The designated zones are to be located in areas of high unemployment or urban decay considered to be in particular need of industrial or commercial investment. The new reliefs consist of 100% tax allowances for capital expenditure on industrial buildings, offices (normally ineligible for any tax allowances) and certain hotels. The reliefs are available, broadly, in relation to expenditure incurred during a period of ten years from the designation of the zone concerned. The precise locations of the zones have not been decided upon although the areas in which they will be situated have been announced.

Ch. 8 **Stock Relief**

Major changes intended to be made to the stock relief rules were announced on 14th November 1980 and are to be effective for all periods ending after that date. Other, favourable changes to the old stock relief rules were enacted in the 1979 and 1980 Finance Acts, but some of these are now of relatively little importance. Precise new rules have still to be formulated but the combined effect of the 14th November 1980 proposed changes and previous changes is expected to be as follows:

a) Clawback of stock relief is abolished, except for circumstances where the level of a firm's stocks is significantly and permanently reduced, for example where a firm ceases business.

   Changes in the law already enacted provide that relief claimed will not be liable to clawback once six years have elapsed from the end of the period in which the relief arose. In addition, stock relief which arose during the first two years for which stock relief could be claimed has already been written off – in most cases this is the relief given for the two accounts years ending next after 5th April 1973 (Paragraph 3 Schedule 3 Finance (No. 2) Act 1979).

   Thus, stock relief is no longer merely a means of *deferring* tax liabilities. Once the relief has been claimed, there will not normally be any risk of a clawback in a future year. In circumstances where a clawback does arise, only relief claimed in the previous six years can be clawed back.

b) Relief will no longer be computed by reference to the increase in stock value over the accounts period. Instead, relief will be calculated as a percentage of the opening stocks for the period concerned. The percentage will be equal to the percentage increase over the period in a special new Government stock price index. The same index will apply to all taxpayers with stocks, regardless of the nature of the business.

The first £2,000 of stocks will be disregarded for the purpose of the new rules; this provision is intended to reduce the number of small claims.

c) For accounts periods commencing after 14th November 1980, where the stocks of a firm (such as a very large partnership) or group of companies exceeds £1M, a new rule, known as the "credit restriction" will reduce the stock relief otherwise available, depending on the extent to which the firm or group of companies is financed by creditors. As this rule will affect only the very largest partnerships, it is not dealt with further here.

d) There will be no deduction by reference to the profits of the firm when computing stock relief under the new rules. Previously, a deduction of 15% (decreased to 10% for accounts periods ending after 5th April 1979) applied to partnerships, referred to on page 107 and subsequently.

e) The new rules will apply for the *full* accounts period starting 14th November 1980. However, transitional rules will allow extra relief in some instances if relief for that period would have been higher under the old rules. In the case of firms with high levels of stock or work in progress at 14th November 1980, it will be advantageous to maintain those levels until after the firm's next accounting date.

f) Fairly complex rules were introduced in the 1980 Finance Act to assist firms which otherwise would have had big tax bills because of temporary reductions in stocks. The long-term need for these rules will disappear because clawback has largely been abolished.

In the shorter term, assuming that the rules are not wholly superseded by the detailed provisions for the abolition of clawback, they will enable the bulk of a clawback chargeable to tax for the tax year 1979/80 (based, for example, on the accounts year to 31st December 1978) to be deferred to 1980/81; for the tax year 1980/81 the stock may have increased again (giving rise to stock relief) so that a heavy tax bill is avoided. It is not possible to predict at this stage how a clawback relating to the tax year 1980/81 will be dealt with as detailed rules have not been announced; however, it is reasonable to expect that special relief will be available.

g) Under rules introduced in 1979, it became permissable to make partial claims to stock relief. Previously, it was necessary to claim all the relief available or none at all. Partial claims will be desirable in some instances where the full amount cannot be effectively utilised, for example, where a partner's personal tax allowances would be wasted if the full stock relief available were claimed. If, following a partial claim, a clawback arises, for example on cessation, the maximum clawback possible will be the relief actually claimed. (Paragraph 2 Schedule 3 Finance (No. 2) Act 1979).

It is likely that when the latest changes to the rules have been finalised, they will include similar provisions about partial claims.

The provisions set out above constitute an outline of the new stock relief rules. As readers may appreciate, the above comments are based to a large extent on proposals which are not yet law and may not be enacted in the precise way expected. Many relatively minor issues need resolving before the new rules become law. There is, however, little doubt that the new rules will in general be enacted in the form described.

p.117 **Overseas Transactions**

The virtual abolition of U.K. exchange controls has removed some difficulties previously associated with overseas transactions.

p.120 **Tax Rates**

Changes to income tax rates are dealt with at the beginning of this Supplement.

p.124 **Class 4 National Insurance Contributions**

For the year ending 5th April 1981, the band of profits on which the 5% charge is calculated is £2,650 to £8,300 (previously £2,250 to £7,000). (S.I. 1979 No. 1694).

pp132-133 **Company Tax Rates**

The lower rate of corporation tax applying to companies with small profits is 40% for the year ended 31st March 1980 and applies to companies with profits less than £70,000. The average rate of corporation tax rises gradually up to 52% where profits are between £70,000 and £130,000. The full rate of 52% applies where profits are in excess of £130,000. The profit figures are reduced proportionately where there are associated companies. (Section 21 Finance Act 1980).

pp135-138 **Shortfall**

The rules have been fundamentally altered so that *trading profits* can no longer generally be apportioned to shareholders in relation to accounts years ending after 26th March 1980. The shortfall rules are now only relevant to companies with other types of income such as interest or rents and some companies whose main activity does not constitute trading. The change in rules is unlikely to have a major impact on partnership service companies as such companies would not normally have sufficiently great profits to give rise to shortfall problems or would otherwise be able to justify retaining their profits. However, the change may make it more attractive for some partnerships to convert into companies. (Section 44 and Schedule 9, Finance Act 1980).

p.157 **Retirement Annuities**

The previous limitations on the maximum deductible premiums have been significantly eased. There is now no overriding cash maximum and the only limitation is that premiums must not exceed 17½% of the income concerned in order to be deductible. The higher percentages applying to persons born in 1915 or earlier are all increased by 2½%.

Major changes have been made to the manner in which the relief is allowed.

(a) Firstly, premiums paid will be deductible for the year during which they are paid or treated as paid. It will be possible to elect to have a premium paid in any year treated as paid in the previous year, or treated as paid in the year before that if no profits were earned in the previous year.

The position under the old rules was broadly that a payment could be deducted for a specific tax year if it was paid within six months after the tax assessment for the year had been agreed, the timing of which could vary considerably.

(b) In future, if less than the maximum deductible premiums are paid in any tax year, the difference can be carried forward for up to six years and correspondingly higher deductible payments made in later years. The higher payments will be deductible in the later years.

(c) If premiums are paid in excess of the maximum amount deductible, the excess cannot be carried forward and it is not deductible in any way or eligible for any of the other tax benefits associated with payments into an approved retirement annuity fund. Since the maximum amount deductible will include unutilised relief for earlier years, as explained in (b) above, the maximum amount may be relatively substantial. In any event, however, great care should be taken to avoid ineligible payments.

The practical implications of the new rules will vary considerably between taxpayers although the general intention of the legislation is to simplify the position and improve the relief available. In particular, for some taxpayers with highly fluctuating incomes who wish to pay substantial deductible premiums, it will probably be necessary to give extra care in this area to ensure that the premiums are deductible in the years when maximum benefits will be obtained. It should also be mentioned that the facility to carry forward unutilised relief will, in some instances, and where desirable, allow substantial tax allowable premiums to be paid in a year of the taxpayer's choice.

The new rules are set out in Sections 31, 32 and 33 Finance Act 1980 and generally are effective for the tax year 1980/81 onwards. The new relief referred to in (b) above, is available for amounts paid less than the maximum deductible for 1974/75 and subsequent years.

p.158 Contributions by a partner towards a conventional endowment policy will attract relief of 15% (previously 17½%) with effect from 6th April 1981 onwards (Section 29, Finance Act 1980).

p.158 **Annuity from the Partners**

The rules concerning the maximum annuity which can be paid to a retired partner (or his dependants) and still be treated as earned income have been changed. The figure (as computed under the old rules) can now be increased by reference to increases in the retail price index (Section 34 Finance Act 1980).